BEYOND THE LECTURE VOLUME 7

CONNOR WHITELEY

Any questions about the book, rights licensing, or to contact the author, please email connorwhiteley@connorwhiteley.net

DEDICATION

Thank you to all my readers without you I couldn't do what I love.

INTRODUCTION

When I first started this Clinical Psychology Reflection series back in 2021, I had no idea that I would ever reach 7 volumes or 140 reflections. Yet I really do love this series because there is only so much information, we can learn in the lecture theatre and in academic textbooks.

I think as aspiring and qualified psychologists, the real learning takes place in the real world. It is by interacting with people, interacting with society and interacting with real-world issues and then reflecting on them through a mental health perspective. That is where we learn the most about clinical psychology and how to help our clients.

I learnt this lesson the best in the past two volumes because Volume 5 focused on me recovering from my child abuse and childhood trauma with other topics added in to keep it light. Then Volume 6 focused on my sexual trauma and the stark mental health and clinical psychology implications of it.

This volume of Clinical Psychology Reflections focuses on a whole host of brilliant topics that I am really excited to share with you. You'll learn a lot about mental health, psychotherapy and clinical psychology giving you extra knowledge and perspectives that you won't find in the lecture theatre or a textbook.

Some of the reflections in this book include:

- Learning from failure in clinical psychology
- Accent as an indicator of socioeconomic status
- Prejudice within clinical psychology
- Sex education and mental health
- Never expect your clients to do something you wouldn't do

And so many more brilliant topics.

This book is perfect for anyone, especially aspiring and qualified psychologists, looking for a fascinating, insightful book written in an easy-to-understand and engaging way.

Who Am I?

Personally, I always love to know who the author is of the nonfiction I read so I know the information is coming from a good source. In case you're like me, I'm Connor Whiteley GMBPsS, the internationally bestselling author of over 50 psychology books.

In addition, I am the host of *The Psychology World Podcast,* a weekly show exploring a new psychology topic each week and delivering the latest psychology news. Available on all major podcast apps and YouTube.

Finally, I am a psychology graduate studying a Clinical Psychology Masters at the University of Kent, England until September 2025.

So now we know more about each other, let's start reflecting on some fascinating clinical psychology topics.

SHOULD AI CHATBOTS BE USED TO TRAIN FUTURE CLINICAL PSYCHOLOGISTS?

Last week, I took part in a new psychology study that a lecturer who I'm friendly with was running and he wanted to conduct his study using clinical psychology master's students. Besides from his preferred research sample, I didn't really know anything else about the research study. Artificial intelligence had been mentioned but besides from that, nothing else was said.

His master's students emailed me a day later and we arranged a date and time to meet. I mention this because here's a little tip, if you are contacting a research participant and you have no idea what they look like and if they have no idea what you look like. Please, do not ask them to meet you in a public space that will be very busy.

Give them a specific room or location. Ideally the place where you're going to be doing the experiment.

Anyway, the study involved me having 12 minutes to ask questions to this chatbot that was pretending to have anxiety and depression. I needed to interact with it how I would with a client in the real-world during the psychological assessment.

I needed to find out their presenting difficulties, their life situation, how long they have had their mental health difficulties amongst other factors.

To do this, I needed to type in my questions to the chatbot and a second or two later, it would give me a response. That answered my question very well and similar to how a real client would answer it with the pauses, nervousness and accurate wording.

When the 12 minutes were up, the researcher came back into the room and she asked me a few questions about my experience, would I recommend using this chatbot in clinical psychology training and how could it be improved amongst other questions.

Personally, I want to reflect on this study because I strongly believe that this will be used in the future of clinical psychology. Artificial intelligence is already dominating and revolutionising our world. For example, there is artificial intelligence baked in all electronic devices these days allowing for smarter, easier and faster search. It might not always be accurate but it is there.

A lot more tools and pieces of software are

incorporating artificial intelligence, businesses are using AI more and more to make work easier and more effective. You cannot escape artificial intelligence.

Even within clinical psychology, artificial intelligence is already being used to deliver psychological therapy as part of mobile mental health apps as I discuss in my book *Could Apps Improve Our Mental Health*? Therefore, it is truly impossible to escape the impact of artificial intelligence on our profession.

Moreover, I do realise that my responses are slightly biased in a way because I am not part of the ideal research sample. The aim of the study I later found out was to see if clinical psychology masters students' opinions on whether this chatbot should be used in professional training.

Nonetheless, it's important that this chatbot should be researched with actual trainee clinical psychologists because they have the training, they have the professional experience and they have the clinical expertise to "truly" judge if this chatbot is remotely effective at developing the psychological assessment skills that qualified clinical psychologists need.

Just a reflective note.

Should Artificial Intelligence Be Used In Clinical Psychology Training?

I'll start off with what I like about this training chatbot. I appreciated how it responded very realistically, similar to how a client would in the real-world. It paused, conveyed nervousness and sometimes the client didn't know how to answer the question I was kindly asking them.

Also, I remember that the majority of answers involved the client picking at the fabric of their sleeve to show that they were nervous. This is similar to what a lot of clients would do in a real therapy session, so I will admit that it's realistic in that sense.

In addition, it was good how the chatbot was a little difficult to get to open up. Similar to working with some clients who you need to find a certain angle or line of questioning before everything starts to flow out of them and you can really start to get to the core of their mental health difficulties.

However, I did have a few issues with the chatbot and this is why I do not believe artificial intelligence and chatbots should be used in clinical psychology training.

Firstly, my issue is that whenever you do psychological assessments, besides from getting certain information that you need from clients, you need to use a range of therapeutic skills. For example, you need to show active listening, you need to respond to what the client is saying so they feel listened to, and you need to phrase your questions in non-judgmental and compassionate ways.

However, the issue with using an AI chatbot is that because I only had 12-minutes to try and get as much information as possible, and I was having to type out each question. After a while, I stopped trying to respond carefully and considerately to what the chatbot was telling me. I was just typing in my questions and asking them.

The chatbot wasn't able to tell this wasn't how I was actually meant to ask questions, because the study wasn't looking at my ability to conduct an effective assessment.

As a result, I don't believe that the chatbot would be useful in developing the interpersonal skills that psychological assessments require, because it doesn't get me to practice how you need to ask them in the real world.

A second issue with the chatbot being used in training is that it doesn't reflect the real world. In a real psychology assessment, even one on video call, I would be able to see the client, read their body language and hear their voice. As well as I would need to think about my body language a lot more because the client would be interpreting my actions too.

Yet a chatbot isn't a real person and whilst the text responses did give me some details about the client's body language, it is one thing to read it and quite another to see it and then reformulate my questions and approach based on that body language feedback. As well as using a chatbot fails to get me to think about my own body language and how I am presenting myself to the client.

These factors could all harm or help the therapeutic alliance to form, and if the client is uncomfortable round me then that will have a large negative impact on the assessment.

Finally, I have a minor issue with how chatbots might be used in the training programmes. As an aspiring clinical psychologist, I want to do the doctorate of clinical psychology because I want to help people, I want to help make the world a better place and I want to improve lives. I can only achieve these aims if I am able to talk and interact with real clients, interacting with a chatbot will not help me.

Therefore, I think there could be a perception issue within clinical psychology. If clinical training providers want to use chatbots as part of training then I think they will need to work on selling this idea to trainee clinical psychologists. They will need to sell them on the idea that chatbots are useful, that chatbots will not take away from their real-world experiences and that the trainees are still going to be getting their money's or time's worth out of the training programme.

Since I believe in the future because of how advanced artificial intelligence is getting, I imagine anyone will be able to get or create a chatbot that can pretend to be a client with depression or anxiety. In this future, this chatbot might be nothing new so in an extreme case, why should people join a doctoral programme to become fully qualified when they can simply use the same artificial intelligence chatbot in the comfort of their own home?

On the whole, I think there is a place for artificial

intelligence in clinical psychology training, but I want us as a profession to be extremely careful. We work with humans so trainees must always get experience with other people before some AI chatbot that will never be as good or useful in the development of the key therapeutic skills that clinical psychologists need.

What do you think?

Should chatbots be used in training or not?

CLASSISM IN ACCESS TO MENTAL HEALTH

I am no stranger to classism and given that I live with a sociology student and someone who is a socialist, I am very familiar with classism and discussions around class structure within society. As well as I am a firm believer in the social constructivist approach to mental health, so again, I like talking about how societal-level factors maintain and play a causal role in mental health difficulties.

However, when I was reading the October 2024 issue of The Psychologist magazine, I was slightly surprised to see an article mentioning that middle-class people are 3 times more likely than working-class people to receive mental health support (Kugelmass, 2016).

Source: Kugelmass, H. (2016). "Sorry, I'm Not Accepting New Patients" an audit study of access to mental health care. Journal of Health and Social Behavior, 57(2), 168-183.

I am not going to lie about my own privilege and my own flaws. The statement shouldn't have surprised me but as a white person who was assigned male at birth, who's straight-passing and no one in the street would know I'm non-binary. I am privileged enough in my life not to experience limits on my access to mental health treatment.

I often pay for my own counselling because private is a lot quicker for me.

Therefore, it shouldn't have been a surprise to me, but it was because of my privilege. I expected middle-class people to be able to afford private mental health support compared to working class, but I was surprised they could access more public support too.

If you're interested in knowing more of the details then definitely check out the article, it's why I included the reference above.

However, I want to reflect on this as a person, as someone who has had more than their fair share of mental health difficulties from trauma, rape and more, and as an aspiring psychologist

As A Person

As a result, as a person, I'm outraged. This is a disgusting finding that really highlights how silly the world is. Your access to mental and physical healthcare is a basic human right, so why does your bank account and your postcode matter?

In the United Kingdom, we are fortunate enough at the time of writing to have a free healthcare service that is world-leading and I am proud of them. As much as I have disagreements with Westminster politics and I have massive issues with the management of NHS England, I am proud to live in a country where I can have these issues.

I am proud to say that the NHS has saved my life as a baby and it is a brilliant service for the most part.

However, the very fact that your class, your income and your socioeconomic status determines your ability to access mental health support is outrageous. That is not the country I want to live in, that is a massive failure because healthcare is for all.

So more work absolutely has to be done to fix this nightmare that means the poorest in our society suffers for no fault of their own.

As A Survivor and Person With Mental Health Difficulties

If you've been a long-term reader of this series, any of my other psychology books or a listener to The Psychology World Podcast, then you might be aware that in my life I have experienced a lot of mental health difficulties over the years for different reasons.

As a result, as a rape survivor and someone who has really struggled with their mental health, I am disappointed in the system. I already knew the system was broken, next to useless and it certainly isn't fit for purpose in the 21st century, but I am disappointed.

I might be from a middle-class family but I come

from a very deprived area. I know how bad the mental health services are in Medway. In fact, I know we sort of have mental health services but they are not the best from what I have heard.

It is because mental health services are so broken and because the rules are you have to have had two believable suicide attempts before a mental health service can see you in the United Kingdom. That I needed to go into private counselling for my childhood trauma, my rape and my anorexia.

I have never been able to get public mental health support and that is sickening.

I am fortunate enough to be able to afford private counselling, but I know there are so many other amazing, innocent and good people who are not able to afford it.

This only perpetuates the health inequalities that we see and makes it easier for middle-class people to get mental health support.

This is wrong because mental health support should be for everyone, and this breaks my heart because I know, I truly know how upsetting and awful mental health difficulties can be.

And the idea that there are so many people struggling in the world, just because of their socioeconomic status being an additional barrier to mental health treatment. That upsets me.

The world deserves better.

As An Aspiring Psychologist

If I think about this as an aspiring psychologist, I

am still outraged but I am able to look at it in a slightly different way. This reflects a lot of things that is wrong with our current mental health system. There are massive health inequalities that mean people near the coast, people in more deprived areas and people who are the poorest in society will always miss out on having access to good mental health support compared to middle-class people.

This is still flat out wrong.

Furthermore, you could argue that this classism is a possible extension of the classism baked into clinical psychology as a profession. Since clinical psychology is a very white middle-class female-dominated profession and it is hard for other people to break into the job market.

With that in mind, you could argue that because of social identity theory and the basic social psychology principle of we like people who are more like us, is it possible that when it comes to selecting new clients, we are more likely to select people who are like us?

For example, other middle-class individuals.

I do not think so but it would be an interesting research question for sure, because all of us have implicit biases that subtly influence our decisions.

On the whole, as an aspiring psychologist, this is something I want to see change and in the future, I would like to be part of this change. Mental health support is for everyone regardless of their race, gender, sexuality, socioeconomic status and more. I know there will unfortunately always be structural inequalities that will maintain the damaging social hierarchy that we have in the world.

Yet even if we can decrease the hierarchy of power and help to decrease some of these health inequalities then that is great progress. And a lot of our clients will be able to benefit now and in the future.

Isn't that all we want? A world where we can help our clients even more.

Getting rid of health inequalities and classism is a brilliant first step.

ACCENT AS AN INDICATOR OF SOCIOECONOMIC STATUS

Source: Levon, E., Sharma, D., Watt, D. J., Cardoso, A., & Ye, Y. (2021). Accent bias and perceptions of professional competence in England. Journal of English Linguistics, 49(4), 355-388.

Building upon the last reflection, I wanted to use our next reflection as a chance to make us all aware of another bias that we have, and mental health organisations have as a whole. When I was reading the October 2024 issue of The Psychologist magazine, I came across the finding of Levon et al. (2022) which found that accent is a primary social signal for socioeconomic status. As well as when I looked into the article in question, I found out it was mainly focused on hiring decisions and perceptions of professional competencies among different professionals in England.

As you can expect the people with accents from traditionally poorer and more deprived areas of England were hired less often than people with accents from richer parts of England.

As a result, in this reflection, I want to reflect on this from three points of view. Firstly, from an aspiring psychologist looking at mental health services. Secondly, as a human who is flawed and I am guilty of making these social judgements because I am not perfect. Finally, I want to think about the people with these accents who are disadvantaged and how this impacts their employability. As well as how we need to be aware of this bias so these people have an equal chance, or more equal chance.

Mental Health Services Hiring

We need to reflect on accent as a social signal from a mental health services point of view, because we need to acknowledge that these services are implicitly going to hire people who they deem as more professionally competent and class plays a role in this decision. I have already mentioned that clinical psychology is a very white middle-class female-dominated profession so it is harder for people of working class to break into the profession.

Partly is because it is more difficult for working class people to take the unpaid work experience opportunities that is needed to gain clinical experience to get paid work within our profession.

This is an inability to get clinical experience because working class people cannot afford unpaid work is a barrier enough. Then there are certain areas of England which are poorer and more deprived than other places. For example, Liverpool, Newcastle, Manchester, the county of Cornwall and so on.

Therefore, when it comes to hiring decisions, we need to make sure that mental health services take a reflective stance on their hiring decisions to see when they reject a client, is it at all possible that it is because of an implicit class-based decision based on postcode, an accent or so on?

Of course, in reality, this would never happen because mental health services are too stretched and there are too many applications to go through to be able to consciously make these decisions for. As well as we risk tokenism and token hires if this policy becomes standard where mental health services only hire people so no one can question if there is systemic classism in the profession.

Which there is.

I talk about the damaging impact of classism in my book, Social Psychology.

On the whole, I do not know the fix that might give people with accents denoting they come from a traditionally poorer area a more equal chance of employment within clinical psychology. Yet we do need to think about it because your region, your accent and your postcode should never determine your ability as a clinical psychologist.

Your core competencies are the only things that should.

Myself As A Flawed Human

Personally, I want to remind myself here more than anything else and I need to be aware of this bias. And I need to make sure in this reflection, I don't come across as someone who is only doing this as lip service or to look good because that isn't why I point out my own flaws. At most, I point out my flaws to show that I am human, I am not perfect and I have a long way to go myself towards being a better person.

Therefore, there have been times when I have made jokes or laughed at jokes and comments without challenging them about classism. As well as certain accents are just horrible. For example, the Liverpudlian accent from Liverpool in the north of England, I have made jokes about how that is an awful accent to try and understand.

Yet in the grand scheme of things, continuing to make accents and where people are come as the butt of jokes without knowing them, it might be damaging. I'll admit another flaw of mine here. I am not well-versed or knowledgeable enough to even pretend to understand the wide-ranging impacts this type of humour probably has but it probably isn't helpful.

Equally, I make lots of jokes about where I am from with Medway being an extremely poor area that is an utter dive to live in. Yet even then I acknowledge that as I mentioned before I am a white person who looks and acts like a cisgender white male who's straight. As well as I come from a middle-income family so I do have a lot of privilege and I have higher social mobility I think than other people in Medway.

Therefore, I know I need to start challenging classism within myself, my family and my wider social community because once classism gets challenged more, and as more people realise that classism is an issue. Then hopefully, one day this can filter through into people's perceptions of professional competencies.

I know this is a very lofty goal and desire, but no one, absolutely no one should be judged or disadvantaged because of their postcode. If I didn't believe in that then I wouldn't be doing as much Outreach work as I do with other students who went to schools in disadvantaged areas like I did.

How Could We Support People With Accents From Typically Poorer Areas?

In my opinion, this reflection was more about awareness because I am not well-versed enough in classism and other inequalities as much as I should be to be able to provide a number of practical solutions to this issue. Yet I think there are some ideas that I can suggest to all of us.

Firstly, whenever you meet a fellow professional and you realise they have a different accent, it might be a good idea to acknowledge this implicit social signal. This will make you aware of it so you can remind yourself if you don't think they are very good at their job or you are vastly better than them. Then as clinical psychologists, it's important that we reflect on ourselves and we can acknowledge is the other person actually bad at their job, or is there a chance I am being prejudiced because of their accent.

I realise this entire reflection will probably rub some people the wrong way but I think it is important that we reflect on our strengths and flaws as aspiring or qualified psychologists, so we can grow as people.

Secondly, we need to challenge this social signal within mental health services so we can help give people with accents from traditionally poor areas a more equal chance of employment within clinical psychology. The profession absolutely has to become more diverse and this is one way to do it.

Speaking of which, one way to help challenge this social signal might be to discuss this finding with your supervisor, so they are aware of it.

Finally, aspiring and qualified psychologists are a community, we are all in this together. Therefore, let's actually support each other. If you know someone who is eager to get into clinical psychology and you're more advantaged than them, then talk to them, point them in the right direction if you know any opportunities that might help them get more experience or take a step closer to becoming a clinical psychologist.

Especially early on in your career, you might think you aren't that advantaged or you might think you don't know any opportunities. Yet I'm mentioning my privilege and I am early on in my clinical psychology career, I still point other students towards work experience placements in the NHS Community Health Trust in Kent, the podcast episode I did on how to get work experience for psychology students on The Psychology World Podcast and so on.

We all know things that will help other people, so let's help others and let's make clinical psychology, the amazing, supportive and wonderful community that I know it is.

A rising tide lifts all ships after all.

NEVER EXPECT YOUR CLIENT TO DO SOMETHING YOU WOULDN'T

In a recent clinical psychology lecture, my lecturer for the following week told us about behavioural activation that she wanted us to do before her lecture next week, then she handed over to our lecturer for this week. She wanted us to complete a behavioural activation worksheet where we noted down our Body, Accomplishment, Social and something we Enjoy each day of the week. Then on the university module page, there was more information on the task.

However, she said something that really stuck with me, she mentioned as aspiring and qualified psychologists, we should never expect our clients to do something if we aren't prepared to do it ourselves.

Personally, I found this a really interesting idea because it is very true. I talk about this in a lot of different spaces because this is why I value lived experience so much within clinical psychology. It is by our lived experience, our shared backgrounds and us going through similar experiences that will allow us to greater empathise with our clients and understand what they're going through.

At some point in this book, I'll explain why lived experience and commitment is actually more important in clinical psychology than the outdated idea of clinical experience.

Anyway, it is very true that we should be willing to do the same things as our clients. Whether this is a worksheet or a behavioural task or even Thought Records. This will allow us to understand how easy or difficult it is and it gives us another point of similarity with our clients.

In addition, in a related area, it is already a requirement for counsellors to undergo counselling for their mental health difficulties. I strongly believe that this should be a requirement for clinical psychologists too.

How are we meant to understand how our client processes therapy if we have never been to therapy ourselves?

As a result, whenever you come across something in your lectures, a textbook or your training, just think to yourself whether this is something you would be prepared to do. If it is something you would be willing to try out, then try it out, learn from it and understand what your clients might struggle with so you can help them overcome the obstacle before setting it.

If the task isn't something you would be prepared to do, then this is a great opportunity to reflect on why. Are you scared about something? Are you nervous about learning something about yourself? Do you think you won't benefit from the task?

Whatever the answer to those questions, every answer is actually rather telling. If you don't think that you would benefit, then chances are you will have a client that thinks that in the future. So show yourself some self-compassion and pretend you're talking to a future client and try to explain why they might benefit so you can realise the benefits too.

In all aspects of our future or current clinical psychology work, we will meet resistance from a client or two. This isn't a bad thing, it just means that we need to explain ourselves better and communicate the benefits and drawbacks of the task with our clients.

In addition, if you're nervous or scared about learning about yourself whilst you do the task. Then you will always have clients who have the same concerns, so see this as a learning opportunity. Practise on yourself and see how you would communicate to a client in this situation. What helpful things could you say to convince them that it is okay to be afraid and concerned and nervous, but this might still be a valuable task to do anywhere.

Just never expect your client to do something you wouldn't do yourself.

Do everything you ask clients to do for yourself and chances are, you're going to learn a lot more than you ever thought possible.

And isn't that half the fun of clinical psychology?

IS THE CLINICAL EXPERIENCE REQUIREMENT OUTDATED?

Whether you're an aspiring or qualified psychologist, you will be well-aware of how clinical psychology works in terms of its infuriating job requirements. To be able to get onto the doctorate of clinical psychology, you need at least one year's clinical experience and typically you get this by working as an assistant psychologist.

At first that sounds perfectly okay because you simply have to get an assistant psychologist position, as well as if you go on any job website then it looks easy. There are tons of different assistant psychologist positions in the United Kingdom, so how hard can it actually be?

In reality, it is very hard to become an assistant psychologist and this makes it even harder to become a fully qualified clinical psychologist.

In addition, becoming an assistant psychologist is difficult enough because the positions are so competitive. Yet they are difficult to get because of another factor too. They require you to already have clinical experience.

That is just confusing, stupid and beyond belief.

You need to become an assistant psychologist so you can get experience, but you cannot become an assistant psychologist without experience. That is just the stupid way how clinical psychology operates.

Of course, you can do unpaid work experience, volunteering with various mental health charities and do other bits and pieces in a small effort to get some clinical experience. Although, if you're a university student then when do you find the time to get this experience? Also, if you come from a lower-income family, area or you have caring responsibilities, can you afford to do unpaid work experience?

This is something I have written a lot about in different volumes of this series, because this is not a solution to the diversity issue that clinical psychology has.

Anyway, in the December 2024 issue of The Psychologist Magazine, there was a very interesting idea put forward about how the clinical experience requirement for the doctorate of clinical psychology might be outdated. The main reason suggested for this is because psychology is actually more about commitment to psychology, but I want to reflect on that statement in the next reflection.

The article included the following quote:

"Even if you land the one assistant psychologist job offer in the country- is it really that vital to becoming a psychologist? Sitting in silence in the room and taking notes while the grown-ups talk- is that really necessary?"

This is what I want to focus on in this reflection because I completely and utterly agree with it. I have worked with assistant psychologists and honestly, I am rather horrified to some extent. Of course, different mental health services will use their assistant psychologists differently.

For instance, I have seen in some assistant psychologist roles that they are nothing more than researchers. This is something that I understand to some extent, but I do not agree with. I understand that assistant psychologists are great researchers because they have knowledge of advanced statistics, research methodologies and they are well-equipped to handle audits and any research that the mental health services need doing.

This is even more important for mental health services like the Gender Identity Clinics in the United Kingdom. And in these particular services, the assistant psychologists perform potentially life-saving research that continues to show the effectiveness of gender-affirming healthcare in reducing psychological distress and improving people's mental health.

However, generally speaking, I do not understand assistant psychologists being glorified researchers. I understand someone has to do it, because the scientist-practitioner model is critical in clinical psychology. Yet people become assistant psychologists to become qualified psychologists.

And I have spoken to a lot of clinical psychologists in the past few years and very few of them are research-focused. In fact, I am fairly sure very few of them know how to conduct good research, because they are so busy juggling caseloads, supervision meetings, Continued Professional Development and so on.

They do not have the time to conduct research even if it is for the mental health service. So this raises the question, why are assistant psychologists being taught research skills instead of actual psychological skills that they can use with future clients?

That is my question.

Moreover, if we go back to the actual quote itself, I have seen assistant psychologists in Multi-disciplinary meetings, and the quote is correct. All that assistant psychologists actually do in these meetings is sit there quietly, take notes and they do not speak.

How is that teaching them valuable therapeutic skills?

You could argue that they are learning by listening and seeing these psychological conversations happen around them with the input of other professions. I would agree with that statement because I do learn things by sitting in on these meetings. And yet, wouldn't I learn the exact same by watching these online through a training programme or university course?

What is so special about me being employed as an assistant psychologist and seeing these conversations?

There is nothing special.

On the whole, at the end of this reflection, I want to stress that the clinical experience requirement for the doctorate of clinical psychology is not well-thought out. Being an assistant psychologist is not critical to becoming a psychologist because most of the time, assistant psychologists are nothing more than glorified researchers or note-takers in meetings.

They do not learn anything critical to becoming a psychologist that you couldn't learn in other ways.

Also, the clinical experience requirement continues to disadvantage people from poorer backgrounds that cannot afford to undertake the unpaid work experience that this requirement demands that we have.

This requirement is unfair, unjust and it is certainly not helping clinical psychology to become the diverse, welcoming and inclusive profession that our clients deserve.

ISN'T CLINICAL PSYCHOLOGY ACTUALLY ABOUT COMMITMENT?

Building upon the last reflection, I want to focus on what was mentioned as the main driving force and requirement of getting onto the doctorate of clinical psychology in the UK. I certainly agree with this statement because it is so true.

Instead of the doctorate requiring you to focus on gaining clinical experience that a lot of people from poorer backgrounds cannot get. And even people from middle-class and higher backgrounds struggle to get because mental health work is so well protected that it often feels like you need to make connections and be in the right place at the right time just to have a shot of gaining some experience. What clinical psychology is actually about is commitment.

This idea of commitment comes in a few different forms but I firmly believe if you take a step back from clinical psychology and truly look at it objectively, everything in our profession comes back to commitment.

Firstly, there is commitment to psychology and learning. You want to study on the doctorate because you want to study psychology even more after your undergraduate and possibly Masters degree. You are committing yourself to three years of extra study and you are wanting to do even more learning as a trainee psychologist. As well as you are committing to continue to learn for the rest of your life through the Continued Professional Development requirements that being a clinical psychologist brings.

To be able to be on the doctorate, you have to be committed to this learning and psychology as a profession.

Therefore, if we take the argument that the clinical experience requirement isn't good (which it is not) then how else can people evidence this commitment to psychology and learning.

Firstly, you could get people to evidence what they do in their free time and their job. For example, what books do they read, who do they follow on social media, how do they continue to engage in psychology, what does their job entail?

Personally, I would love to use The Psychology World Podcast and my books as evidence as commitment to learning and psychology. Every single week without fail since the 11th November 2019, I have produced a psychology podcast episode focusing on a different area of psychology so I can keep learning.

Shouldn't this help me to become a psychologist?

It shows that I am committed to learning about psychology even when I don't have to. My podcast isn't going to get me a qualification, a ton of money or a legion of adoring fans (even though if you are a podcast listener. Thank you. You are amazing), so I am effectively doing the podcast for free and I have no intention of stopping.

That is surely the definition of commitment.

Of course, other aspiring psychologists wouldn't want to produce a podcast to show their commitment to psychology. Yet it should be evidenced in other ways like reading every issue of The Psychologist, a given journal or doing research projects for fun outside of their course requirements.

Secondly, the clinical psychology doctorate is actually about our commitment to our clients. It is about our commitment to wanting to improve lives, decrease psychological distress and help our clients develop more adaptive coping mechanisms.

That is the clinical psychology mandate as I call it.

As a result, this could be evidenced by how passionate, determined and driven someone is to become a psychologist and help others. If someone is determined to help clients improve their mental health then they will be good students because you are giving them more ways to help people. That is actually what they want and these students who just want to help people will be just as good as people with clinical experience.

Both types of people are committed to supporting our clients every day.

This could be evidenced by their volunteering, how passionate their cover letters and their interview answers are, and there are other ways to tell how passionate people are about helping clients too.

None of these evidencing ways are perfect but I want to show you that there are other ways to show that aspiring psychologists deserve a place on the clinical psychology doctorate than how much experience they have.

Finally, clinical psychology is about our commitment to the National Health Service and each other as a profession. Whenever you talk to a psychologist, they are committed to supporting other people in our profession. Whether this is other psychologists or physiotherapists, speech and language therapists, occupational therapists and on and on.

Psychology doesn't have all the answers and none of the other professions do either. It is only by working together that we can improve clients' lives the most and that is why we must always be committed to supporting each other.

In terms of how this could be evidenced, commitment to each other and the organisation could be evidenced by proof of working in large organisations with lots of policies. Since that highlights the aspiring psychologist can handle the nightmare of large organisations like the National Health Service. Yet working in supportive roles could be a good way to evidence this commitment too.

Ultimately, at the end of this reflection, I hope that you've started to realise that clinical psychology really isn't about the amount of experience you have working with people with mental health difficulties. Of course, that is a good and important part of clinical psychology.

But it is not the only way, and I firmly believe no one, absolutely no one should be disadvantaged or stopped from becoming a qualified psychologist because they cannot get this experience.

There are so many great aspiring psychologists that might never become qualified because of this outdated, damaging and ill-informed requirement.

Change needs to happen and this could be an important part of that change and improving our profession for the betterment of clients.

IMPORTANCE OF HAVING A PLAN B IN YOUR PSYCHOLOGY JOURNEY

"Don't get so invested in it, have a Plan B. Take the pressure off yourself,"- Dr Charlie Jones

In the grand scheme of things, it is very rare for me to find a quote that I am passionately interested in and it really hits home, but when I do find a quote I like, I really like it. This happened when I was reading the July and August 2024 issue of The Psychology Magazine because there was an article explaining how there is no shame in having a backup plan.

In fact, it is strongly recommended that you have a backup plan because not everyone will be able to become a psychologist. It is very competitive, you need a lot of experience and it is not easy to break into. Sometimes becoming a fully qualified clinical psychologist appears like a lottery. Even more so when it comes to applying for the Doctorate of

Clinical Psychology.

Personally, in my own cohort, both at undergrad and postgrad, I see so many students and aspiring psychologists putting so much pressure on themselves. They stress about grades, they stress about understanding the course content and they stress about making sure they are in the best possible position to increase their chances of becoming a clinical psychologist.

They focus on these aspects so much so that they lose the enjoyment.

Of course, I am not saying that you shouldn't focus on these aspects. It is important to your future career that you focus on getting good grades, you understand the course content and you do the best you possibly can. Yet it is not the end of the world, I've written before about the importance of having fun on your clinical psychology journey and I still stand by that.

Your time at university and the early stages of your clinical psychology career should be a fun time filled with opportunities, learning and you growing as a person. If you are constantly stressed and worried about becoming this one type of professional then it is little wonder that you aren't going to enjoy it.

Therefore, it's important that you check in with yourself about your journey. Ask yourself the questions below:

- Are you enjoying your psychology journey?

- Are you stressing, focusing and/ or worrying too much about your journey?
- If you are, how could you bring more enjoyment into your psychology journey?

Personally, I have struggled with this at various points in my psychology journey. Part of my stress was rape-related because I was so sensitive to hearing about mental health challenges that I would start breaking down and having a full-on mental health crisis of my own if I was exposed to other people's mental health difficulties.

However, even now, I am always a little concerned about my ability to become a clinical psychologist. Especially, because my research experience is packed but in terms of clinical work, I am struggling so much to get experience. I won't repeat myself too much because I've written about it in different places before, but getting clinical psychology work experience is so hard.

If I don't become a clinical psychologist, I think it will mainly be because of my struggle to get experience.

In addition, I could let this struggle compound my concern, make me fearful for the future and my mental health could dip because of this concern. Yet because I have other plans in place if I don't get to become a psychologist, I am okay.

Sure, I would flat out love to become a psychologist and I fully intend to do almost anything in my power to become one. Yet I am grateful that I have other plans in place just in case, because it really does help take the pressure off.

If you're interested in learning more about all the different opportunities that a psychology degree gives you, then please check out my book *Careers In Psychology* available anyway you got this book from.

In addition, to becoming an author, my other options if I can't become a clinical psychologist includes:

- Assistant psychologist
- Wellbeing practitioner
- Private counsellor
- Children's counsellor
- Rape counsellor
- Speech and language therapist
- Forensic psychologist
- Academic researcher
- And more

I came up with those ideas in about a minute and I know there are a lot of other career options for me if I thought about it even longer.

Personally, I love that there are so many options available to me. Not only because it shows if you have a psychology degree then there are a lot of transferable skills that the majority of employers will be looking for. Yet it means that I can take the pressure off myself, I can show myself some compassion and I don't have to be constantly stressed about the chance of never being a clinical psychologist.

I would love to be a clinical psychologist but if I can't become one, then it is not the end of the world. There are plenty of other great jobs that I would do and most importantly, enjoy.

Ultimately, my point is whether you are currently enjoying your psychology journey or not, please start thinking about possible back-up options for yourself. This isn't about you giving up on your dreams, it really isn't. Instead, this is about protecting your mental health, your stress levels and your enjoyment of one of the best journeys you're ever going to have in your life.

Focus on enjoying your psychology journey instead of stressing about your future career, and you'll probably find your mental health, your life and your future self will only get better.

MY EXPERIENCE OF THE FAILED SEX EDUCATION SYSTEM

In the next few reflections, we're going to focus on sex education and sex amongst young people. Especially amongst teenagers. Please note, this is going to be based on content from the October 2024 issue of The Psychologist magazine, and the age of consent in the United Kingdom is 16 years old.

Yet before we dive into the thought-provoking ideas and comments from The Psychologist magazine, I wanted to talk about my experiences of the sex education system. It is awful, useless and it does not prepare anyone to actually have sex. Especially, minority groups and it fails heterosexuals in a lot of different ways.

Why Does Good Sex Education Matter?

In case, like me, you aren't fully aware about why good sex education is so important, allow me to explain why this is critical to us, our young people and society. Good sex education allows children and young people to have the values, skills, knowledge and attitudes that help them to protect themselves, their health and the rights of other people.

In addition, good sex education teaches children and young people how to have respectful sexual and social relationships, as well as make responsible choices.

In the next few reflections, we'll focus more on the idea of responsible choices with a concept called "condom negotiation". That is a fascinating concept for sure.

However, as you'll see in the rest of this chapter, my sex education experience didn't teach me how to protect myself, my rights and how things worked. Maybe if sex education was better, my rapist could have avoided me or hell, my rapist might not have needed to rape people to have sex because he's a monstrous dickhead.

Finally, there are two reasons why I am putting sex education in a psychology book. Firstly, as I explain in *Biological Psychology*, sex is a primal drive and it is a behaviour so it firmly falls in the remit of psychology. Especially as romantic and sexual relationships are part of mainstream social psychology.

Also, if people are not taught healthy, respectful relationships then this can have extremely negative impacts for their mental health. For example, rape can lead to depression, Post-Traumatic Stress Disorder, suicidal ideation and more.

Sex education is another facet of mental health to some extent.

On the whole, the system is failing to protect our young people and children because it is not teaching them what they need to know to have respectful relationships and good sex.

<u>My Experiences Of Sex Education</u>

Personally, there are only three real sex education experiences that I had at secondary education so between the ages of 12 years old and 18 years old. In those six years, I remembered being a 12-year-old and at the end of primary school having a lesson on condoms. Yet this is England so it was very vague and no details were discussed.

In all honesty, that lesson for 12-year-olds was more so the female members of the year group could go into another room and learn about periods and how to put on a tampon or pad. Since in a few years they would be starting their periods.

However, I was recently talking to a female friend of mine and she raised the point saying men should also learn about periods, tampons and pads too. She argued that the majority of men are going to get with women who are going to be dealing with it every month, so surely they should learn about it so they can understand it, empathise and know what the woman is going through every month.

I always say that I'm never going to need the

information about periods, because I'm gay. Yet I still think it would be useful to be aware of periods and what women go through every month. As well as I've discovered in the past year that I am perfectly happy to date a transmasculine person or transman and these people still experience periods pre-transition, so I might get with someone who has periods in the future.

It would be useful information to be aware of.

The Second Experience

My second experience of sex education was probably when I was around 16 years old and it was about consent. Now, as a rape survivor, I have massive issues with how consent is taught in schools but more on that point in a moment. I am seriously not happy.

Anyway, when I was in secondary school, this was when the "Tea" video was popular. If you have not had the enjoyment of watching the Tea video, it is basically the butt of most young people's jokes at this point. It uses the idea of a cup of tea as consent.

For example, just because your friend wanted "tea" yesterday, doesn't mean they want "tea" right now. In other words, just because you had sex last night, doesn't mean you get to have sex right now without asking.

As a young autistic person, I did not understand that video and I needed someone to explain it to me in more depth. For my autistic mind, it was a little too abstract but I fully understand it now.

Now my issue with that damn video is that it talks about consent in the most unhelpful and stupid way possible. This describes consent as simply asking if it's okay to have sex, but consent in the real world is so much more.

You can ask to have sex with someone and if they say yes. It is not a simple case of having sex because you need to get consent throughout it like touching, doing certain things and you need to make sure that your partner is actually happy to have sex. And that they aren't simply saying yes out of fear or because they don't want to upset you.

There is so much more to consent, sex and healthy relationships than simply saying yes or no.

This is why enthusiastic consent is so important and this is what should actually be taught in schools. Here's a definition of enthusiastic consent:

"Enthusiastic consent is a way for you and your partner to give and get sexual consent by communicating, either physically or verbally, your needs and desires before and during any type of sexual activity. That's the enthusiastic consent definition, plain and simple.

At the end of the day, you want a sexual partner who is engaged and having fun rather than being passive and disinterested. Practising enthusiastic consent is a natural way to ensure everyone involved is having a good time when you want to engage in sexual activity. Plus it's really easy – just check in with your partner every now and again to keep things enjoyable and sexy."

Source- TheMix.Org.Uk

Again, as a rape survivor, when I went into fawn mode and I just froze so he continued doing everything to me. I didn't know about enthusiastic consent and clearly he didn't either. He couldn't see that I wasn't enjoying it, that I was scared and I was disinterested. Granted, he would not have cared but this is what our young people and children should be taught.

They should be taught that during sex and healthy sexual relationships enthusiastic consent is the gold standard and it should be the norm.

In fact, I've recently entered my first relationship and I'm excited to have sex at some point. Consensual sex for the first time in my life and the saddest thing is that my rape and recovering from my sexual trauma has taught me more about healthy sex than sex education ever did.

How sad is that?

That I needed to get raped to learn what healthy sex was. If that isn't a damning sentence against the failed state of the sex ed system then I don't know what is.

Sex Education Fails LGBT+ People

Back in secondary school, there was another assembly on sex education but it was so unremarkable and no one learnt anything. Yet there was one comment I remembered, the woman doing the talk mentioned "I'm sorry to all the gay people in the room but this talk is aimed at straight people as they're the majority". It was something like that and honestly, that is a major factor that makes sex education so useless.

In addition, this goes back to my thoughts earlier about why men might find it helpful to learn about women's monthly experiences so they can understand and empathise. Why can't straight people learn about LGBT+ sexual health even briefly?

I have to learn about straight sexual health constantly even though I am never going to use it. And if straight people did learn about LGBT+ sexual health then it could increase acceptance and it could actually combat a lot of the myths in society about how unsafe gay sex is.

Especially, as HIV is actually more common in straight people these days compared to the LGBT+ community.

Source-
https://www.tht.org.uk/news/heterosexual-hiv-diagnoses-overtake-those-gay-men-first-time-decade

Even if LGBT+ sex education was mandated for only LGBT+ people then a large chunk of people wouldn't be able to attend. For instance, if my school had offered it, I would still have to go to the straight sex ed talk because I was so in fear for my life that I couldn't risk people knowing I was gay. I flat out couldn't risk my parents finding out I was gay so again, this would not work.

Therefore, this is another way how the sex

education system is failing our children and young people because it is not allowing LGBT+ individuals to learn how to have healthy and respectful social as well as sexual relationships and how to protect themselves.

More has to be done so everyone, whether you're straight or gay, can be protected, empowered and have fun sex.

Isn't that all we want in life?

MENTAL HEALTH AND CONDOM NEGOTIATION AMONGST ADOLESCENTS

There are certainly particular topics that really show and highlight to myself, my friends and the entire world how ignorant I am about perfectly normal topics, as well as these same topics highlight just how much my childhood trauma has impacted my life. Since until I read the October 2024 issue of The Psychologist magazine, I had no idea whatsoever that condom negotiation was even a thing amongst youth (and people of any age).

I just thought that everyone wanted to use condoms because that's what we're taught in sex education classes. Even though as I mentioned in the last reflection, sex education classes are next to useless, so I suppose I should have known better than to think condoms would always be used.

However, the more I read about condom negotiation, the more surprised I was that there were strategies typically teenage boys used to make their female partner agree to not using a condom. Then there were different strategies that the teenage girl would use to make their boyfriend or sex partner use a condom with them.

The reason why I'm writing about this in a clinical psychology book is because some of the strategies used by teenage boys against girls are abuse, violence and emotional manipulation as well as coercive control. This clearly has a negative impact on their mental health so it is important that we are aware that this is something teenagers can go through.

In addition, teenage boys don't have a perfect time either. Partly because of the strategies used against them but because of the teenage culture surrounding sex. For example, there is often peer pressure in my experience to have sex and lose your virginity because it makes you a "man" amongst other negative aspects of male culture.

All these social and cultural factors impact our mental health to various degrees and that's why aspiring and qualified psychologists need to be aware of them.

Personally, I think there are three main reasons why I am so surprised by the existence of condom negotiation. Partly, this is shaded for me because my rapist never gave me the choice of a condom so I must have formed an implicit association between consensual sex always uses a condom (unless for reproductive purposes) and rape is without a condom.

Even though now I write that paragraph, I realise nothing could be further from the truth. Yet this is one of my own biases.

Another reason why I was surprised by condom negotiation is because I thought everyone would want to use a condom, because it is what you are *meant* to do according to sex educators. And with me being a virgin at the time of writing, I have never experienced not wanting to use a condom.

Finally, I have never had to have this conversation or read about teenage sexual relationships, so honestly I have no idea how this stuff works.

Yet as my housemates pointed out, they are well aware that condom negotiation is a thing with one of them saying something along the lines of "teenage boys don't like condoms because *it* (penetrating a vagina) doesn't feel real when using a condom.

To say I learnt something right there and then is an understatement.

What Are Some Pro-Condom Strategies?

Obviously, in sexual relationships, there will always be people who want to use condoms and those who do not want to use condoms and this is especially true in teenage sexual encounters and relationships when they are still learning what the hell they're doing. This is largely a failure of the useless sex education system as we explored in the last reflection.

Therefore, to generalise here because this is still true for gay and lesbian sexual encounters, when one partner wants to use a condom but the other person (typically a guy) doesn't want a condom, the teenage girl uses a number of strategies to encourage their boyfriend or sex partner to use a condom.

Firstly, a girl can use emotional coercion to encourage her boyfriend to use a condom. This can be done through "playing on his heart strings". As well as the girl could present risk information to her boyfriend to make him want to use a condom so they don't get a Sexually Transmitted Infection, pregnancy concerns amongst others.

Two other strategies a girl can use to encourage the use of a condom involve withholding sex and promising rewards for him using a condom.

From a mental health perspective, using a condom when one person doesn't want to makes the girl feel a lot better, more positive and it helps to remove some of the stressors surrounding sex. Especially, if this is their first time because let's face it, the girl has more to lose than the boy. If the boy doesn't use a condom then the girl can get pregnant which could potentially have a lifetime of consequences for her.

Therefore, if the boy doesn't use a condom then this can have a lot of stress on the sexual encounter, which as you'll see in the next reflection takes away the pleasure and agency aspects of sex. These are very important to having enjoyable sex that focuses on the fun.

Therefore, these strategies can be an effective way that young boys and girls manage to get their partner to use a condom when they don't want to. Then this helps to protect their mental health a little more by removing the stressors of getting a sexually transmitted infection or getting pregnant. As well as since condom use increases the agency and pleasure of the girl then this helps to decrease the chance of sexual trauma occurring in this situation.

What About Anti-Condom Use?

On the other hand, whilst the teenage girl might be using the pro-condom strategies to encourage their boyfriend to use a condom, their boyfriend will be using anti-condom strategies too. These strategies are largely the same as the pro-condom strategies because a boy can use emotional coercion to encourage their girlfriend that it's okay not to use a condom. They might say not using a condom feels better, it's more fun and it makes for better sex.

In addition, the teenage boy might withhold sex or offer his girlfriend a reward for letting him not use a condom. And he might represent his girlfriend with risk information. For example, he doesn't have any sexually transmitted diseases, it's perfectly safe and nothing bad is going to happen if they don't use a condom.

Up until that point, the pro- and anti-condom strategies are very similar.

However, there are more extreme anti-condom strategies, like physical violence and sexual trauma. Since if a teenage boy really doesn't want to use a condom then one horrific option is just ignore what his girlfriend said and just have sex with her regardless of whether she wants him to use a condom or not.

Personally, I flat out hate anti-condom strategies. It largely comes from the fact that my rapist didn't use a condom and it was even more traumatising, it gave my Post-Traumatic Stress Disorder something powerful to latch onto and it is hell. I was scared of catching something off him and I was terrified.

It only made the sheer trauma of my rape even worse.

Therefore, physical and sexual violence is wrong on so many levels and it should never ever happen. I am somewhat okay with the other anti-condom strategies but violence should never ever be used.

And this is why we need a better sex education system so young boys and girls truly know that this is not okay under any circumstances. They need to understand why condoms are important, why protection and consent are critical in healthy sexual relationships.

If both people agree not to use a condom then that is somewhat okay, but if one person says no then the other person should always, always respect it no matter what.

Consent, agency and pleasure are the three most

important aspects of sex and that is what we'll explore now in the next reflection.

WHAT IS THE SO-CALLED SEX POSITIVITY MOVEMENT AND HOW DOES IT PROTECT YOUNG PEOPLE?

In the past two reflections, we've focused on sex education and teenagers as well as young people having sex. Sometimes this is the first time or this is part of their regular relationship. We have learnt about condom negotiation and how the strategies used can damage mental health and put young people at risk. As well as we've learnt about the failures of the sex education movement.

Therefore, in this final reflection on sex and sex education, I want to focus on the approach to sex education that is so-called "The Sex Positivity Movement". And as the October 2024 issue of The Psychologist magazine mentions:

"The approach recognizes sex as a normal and healthy part of adolescent development, and three key priorities are pleasure, consent and agency."

In addition, being sex positive is not about risk. This isn't about encouraging people to take sexual risks, instead it is focusing on sex being a healthy and normal part of adolescent development.

The reason why I really like this approach is because the current system is not working, and as I discussed two reflections ago. The current sex education system is harming children by not teaching them about sex, not teaching them about how to have healthy and consensual relationships and it is putting people at risk of abuse and sexual violence.

Largely, this is because as a society, especially in the United Kingdom, we are too scared to openly talk about sex with young people and even each other and our friends. It is this culture of silence around sex that is creating and reinforcing the dangers around sex and relationships.

Here's the thing. Adolescents and young people will find out what relationships about sex one way or another. They will go online, read God knows what articles from what sources and they will watch porn or other material to learn how to have sex and have relationships.

We have all seen online and read the dangerous, sexist and harmful articles that preach that women are property and women should be treated in a certain way because that is what they deserve.

Do we really want our teenagers and young people learning what relationships that way?

No, we do not.

Equally, do we really want adolescents and young people to learn about relationships and sex through pornography?

Porn is not realistic, it is not reflective of the real world and sure, it *might* teach a young man or woman how to physically have sex. Yet from what I understand about sex, there is way more to sex than that.

There is the emotional, psychological and tender side of sex that can bring two people together. I was talking about my perception of sex with my partner the other night because we're thinking about having sex (I'm a virgin, they are not) and we both agreed that sex isn't cheap and meaningless, but it isn't a great soul-bonding experience either.

Porn will never ever teach adolescents and young people about that side of sex. As well as porn will never teach them about the importance of consent and agency either.

If we do not teach our children and young people how to have healthy sexual relationships that rely on consent, pleasure and agency where both (or more) parties have complete control over what's happening to them. Then only bad things will happen like sexual violence, trauma and abuse.

Is that what we want as individuals? As friends? As parents? As a society?

The Solution

As a result, the solution to protect teenage boys

and girls and young people is to break the silence and shyness that we have about sex in society. This isn't about encouraging young boys and girls to have sex at an early age, it is about accepting that the vast majority of teenagers want to have sex at that age.

This is a normal and healthy part of teenage development and teenage sex will happen whether we want it to or not. Therefore, as a society, educators and as mental health professionals, it is our duty to give young people the tools, knowledge and skills that they need to be able to have sex safely, consensually and make it fun without having to resort to sexual violence, abuse or trauma as we explored in the last reflection.

By talking more openly about sex, we're allowing young people to understand what consent actually is instead of that stupid tea video that really doesn't capture the meaning of consent in the slightest. In the real world, consent is so much more than a simple yes or no. Consent is a lot more complex, it can change and be withdrawn at any moment and that's okay.

If we don't have real conversations about sex then young people will not know this and this is how the risk of sexual violence occurring increases.

By not talking about consent and teenage sex openly, we are leaving the door wide open to sexual trauma because people just do not understand what consent is, and how they should always, always be fully in control of their actions during sex (also known as agency) and sex should always be fun.

In my experience, when I was raped, even though I am firmly of the belief that rape is not sex in the slightest. My sexual encounter never should have taken away my consent, never should have stripped me of my agency and it should have been pleasurable.

My rape was none of those things, but at the time like a lot of other sexual violence survivors, I did not know that I was raped until the next day when my body was telling me something was extremely wrong.

If I had been allowed to have more sex conversations with educators, friends and so on before my rape, I might have understood at the time what was happening and maybe I could have changed something.

Yet as I remind myself often, sexual violence is never your fault because you couldn't have prevented it.

On the whole, the so-called sex positivity movement recognises that teenage sex is a healthy and normal part of adolescence that focuses on giving people the knowledge, skills and understanding so sex is always about consent, agency (being in control of your actions and what's happening to you) and pleasure.

Sex should always be pleasurable for everyone involved.

As well as it protects our young people because they will have sex whatever happens. Teenagers will still have sex whether it is legal or illegal, whether they know what they're doing or not, or whether they understand consent or not and that is where sexual violence comes in.

The less we talk about healthy, consensual sex, the greater risk we are putting on young people because they will not understand the complexities of sex in the real world. They will not understand what consent actually involves and they will not understand how pleasure must always be a focus of sex.

This is where the current sex education system is failing, and ultimately harming our young people.

It is time to break the silence around teenage sex and accept that it is a normal and healthy part of adolescence.

And if we really want to protect our young people and decrease the cycle of sexual violence that is happening every day against boys and girls, it is time to teach our young people what healthy, positive and consensual relationships are.

And why they are some of the most amazing things you can ever experience.

WHY AM I TRYING ANXIETY MEDICATION?

This might actually be one of the most shocking reflections I have ever written because I am a stalwart believer in the issues of the biomedical model, as well as I have massive issues with the medical doctors giving biological solutions as a first-line treatment for mental health conditions. Especially, as the research is so limited and poor when it comes to the science behind anti-depressant.

As focused on in the brilliant academic paper Read and Moncrieff (2022) that annihilated the biomedical model's argument for using anti-depressants to treat depression.

Furthermore, my main issue with the biomedical model is how the medical system uses anti-depressants not because they are helpful, long-term treatments for people with depression and anxiety.

Instead the healthcare system in the UK uses anti-depressants because they are cheaper than giving people psychological therapy.

That is outrageous in my opinion because whilst I fully understand that the National Health Service is a business that must make cost-effective decisions so its limited budget that is already destroyed each year by managerialism, can help as many people as possible.

Giving psychological therapy to everyone who needs it would be extremely cost-effective because it would help a lot more people than anti-depressants ever could. Because anti-depressants only treat the non-existent biological causes of depression (Read and Moncrieff, 2022) whereas psychological therapy helps to treat the biased cognitive processes, the social factors and how people react to different situations, as well as CBT can help people to unlearn the maladaptive coping mechanisms that they have developed.

Anti-depressants cannot.

So why have I decided to start taking anxiety medication?

My Reasons

Between my childhood abuse, my rape and all the friendship trauma I endured because of my undiagnosed autism and the social world I lived in, my nervous system is constantly on fire so much so that I do not notice it. Yet I have had lots of conversations with good friends recently and they've pointed out I am always anxious and I am memorable because I am always awkward.

Something that actually surprised me.

If we use silly functioning labels that I flat out hate but they are good for illustrative purposes. I have high-functioning anxiety because I am able to do so much with my life, I am able to connect with people and so on, but my past trauma means there is always a lot of underlying anxiety with me.

I don't even realise it most of the time.

In addition, I know I'm anxious all the time because whilst my window of tolerance is big, when certain things start to pile up. I get super scared, anxious and I get very distressed.

For instance, for the past two days I've been rather physically ill with a lack of sleep and malnourishment (at the time I thought I had been eating enough this week) then last night, me and some friends were playing Dungeons and Dragons and I was going to do a roleplaying thing which would have been fun in-game, but as a psychology person, it would not be okay. Then one of my friends at the table told me off for wanting to do it where no one else at the table cared because it's a game and I was cartoonish.

This made me very anxious and I started to shut down because I didn't know how to react to my friend's harsh reaction. And the Dungeons and Dragons session basically became a mini-therapy session for him anyway because of the themes and his own past trauma.

Then I started to get distressed and anxious about me seeing another friend today who I asked out this week and they haven't replied to my message. To be honest, I suspect it's going to be a no but I don't want to lose them as a friend because we get on great, so I was anxious about that.

Finally, I was so exhausted and sick last night and it really does show that I am always anxious about things.

Which was why Wednesday morning (three days ago at the time of writing) I filled out an e-consult form with my medical doctor and the next day he phoned me back. We completed the depression and anxiety sub-scales of the DASS-21 (I only knew it because I use it for my research) and he said I had significant anxiety and mild depression.

Honestly, the anxiety responses were honest but I will admit that the depression cores might have been exaggerated on my part, because I wanted access to medication and with medical doctors in the UK (and everywhere else to be fair) you need to make yourself sound worse than you are if you want any kind of help.

Therefore, I think it's interesting to reflect on because I should have told the truth, but it is a sad reflection of the dire state of healthcare in the UK that people feel like they need to lie about their mental and physical health just to get support. As well as whilst I know gatekeeping is important when the

NHS is under such extreme pressure and strain, this could be dangerous because if people are making themselves out to be worse than they are then doctors might give them the wrong medication and so on.

Just something to think about, but that's why I always prefer psychological support over medication.

To my surprise, the doctor did actually offer me Talking Therapies on the NHS, but I already have counselling and she uses some CBT techniques. As well as I have so much trauma and things to work through, 6 sessions on the NHS will not be enough. I would rather pay for private counselling (even though I would love private therapy but that is so expensive) and let someone from a poorer background have my sessions.

And the waiting list would be stupidly long anyway.

Yet the doctor provided me with medication without hesitation afterwards.

As a result, he gave me escitalopram, a Selective Serotonin Reuptake Inhibitor (SSRI) for depression and anxiety. For a week I need to take 5mg then I need to go up to 10 mg and because this is the same stuff my housemates are on (because we all go to the same doctor) I know what to expect.

Ultimately, I wanted to go on anxiety medication because psychological support, including specialist rape counselling, has helped me tons in decreasing my anxiety because I am actually able to function, live my life and be happy. Yet I am desperate for support to decrease my baseline level of anxiety.

I am sadly willing to try medication to see if this can have any benefits and if this can help me.

Me going on escitalopram is more out of desperation than an actual want.

My Reflections On The Process

Personally, I am surprised that I was given this medication this easily because this is not how mental health support is meant to work. Anti-depressants and anxiety medication is meant to be for people with mental health conditions, I have not been diagnosed, I have never been assessed or anything.

Moreover, when we consider that the biomedical model flat out loves their precious DSM-5 that makes it very easy for people to get diagnosed with depression and anxiety so they can go on to medication. It makes me question why is it medication first and not assessments and diagnosis.

Besides the fact that it allows Big Pharma to make billions, why are we just giving out medication to anyone who says they have depressive or anxiety symptoms?

That is not how healthcare is meant to work.

Why is it for depression and anxiety you can get a 10-minute phone call and get medication? Whereas if I am making myself physically sick for weeks because I have anorexia, why can I not get support for that considering anorexia is one of the deadliest mental health conditions known to us?

It is all because there is no money in anorexia

treatment.

I am sure that some readers will have massive issues with what I'm saying, but I think that's a good thing. It is good to be challenged and it's why I comment on the biomedical arguments from time to time, because being challenged is good. It helps us to think critically and it helps us to become more informed mental health professionals.

Something that our clients absolutely deserve.

WHY SHOULD US PSYCHOLOGISTS KNOW BETTER?

There are a lot of myths and misconceptions that I flat out hate within psychology, and some of these myths are repeated by psychologists but a lot of other myths are repeated by laypeople outside of psychology.

I recently came across and experienced one of the most damaging psychology myths in my opinion. It is the myth that because we are experts in psychological theory and mental health, we must know better than our clients, other people and we must be experts in treating our own mental health.

It was reading about this myth in the December 2024 edition of The Psychologist magazine that me realise that I wasn't the only person experiencing this awful myth.

Back in November 2024 during the tail end of

my horrific mental health caused by my rape, I was really struggling with some social relationships and my rape was combining with it to make me extremely distressed, anxious and I wasn't in a good place. So my best friend thinking they had some life experience and lessons to teach taught me some things about myself that I didn't like.

And then they mentioned surely I should have learnt about these trauma responses and how trauma impacts a person's life in my lectures and through my psychology degree.

Personally, that made me even more distressed because I know my best friend was not trying to be uncompassionate or harsh. Yet to me, they were implying that I wasn't being a good aspiring psychologist, that I wasn't as good as I needed to be and it just showed such a lack of understanding about just how massive psychology is as a subject.

My best friend studies physics which is just as massive as psychology to be fair.

Therefore, when my mental health was a bit better and my anorexia got worse because of the distress of this conversation (and the so-called lessons my friends taught me about myself but I talk more about this in *Healing As A Survivor),* I realised I was angry with my best friend.

I was so annoyed that my best friend thought just because I study psychology, just because I focus on mental health and just because I live and breathe clinical psychology that it must make me an expert.

And I have to know everything and be able to apply it to my own life.

No, this is not how the real world works.

Yes, through my books, my podcast and my degrees, I know a lot about mental health as well as psychotherapy but I am not an expert. To me, you can only really become an expert when you're fully qualified after the doctorate of clinical psychology.

In addition, psychologists are still human at the end of the day. We all have our own blind spots, we all have our own faults and just because we can help the mental health of our amazing clients. It doesn't mean that we are able to apply all our psychological knowledge, our techniques and our therapeutic skills to ourselves.

Honestly, I think this is largely because when you have mental health difficulties, this leads to biased cognitive processes. Therefore, of course, you aren't going to be able to apply your therapeutic knowledge to yourself because depending on the mental health difficulties you're experiencing, they will distract and stop you from working at your best.

For example, when I was suffering from the worst of my Post-Traumatic Stress Disorder, most of the minutes of every hour of every day, I was too distressed, I was too terrified and I was reliving my trauma over and over so I couldn't apply any of my degree and knowledge to my situation. The same was true when I was experiencing the depression that comes along with PTSD, I was able to use some techniques but I felt so down, so useless and everything took so much energy that it meant these techniques were only so effective.

In addition, as people within psychology will know, therapy and improving your mental health is an interpersonal process. You will always have a therapist or mental health professional, your social support network and so on. You cannot heal from trauma, mental health difficulties or anything alone.

Therefore, the very notion that psychologists should know better because they are experts in theory, and they shouldn't need mental health support is just beyond stupid.

We will always need the mental health support of other professionals. This doesn't make us weak, silly or bad psychologists. It just means that we are human and that is flat out critical because our clients are humans, so this helps us and our clients see that we are relatable to them. Us psychologists are not perfect, we are not gods and we are not better than them.

And once we realise that and we show our clients our humanity, then that removes one extra barrier from building a successful therapeutic alliance.

On the whole, yes I know a whole bunch of techniques, therapies and skills from everything I do but no, it does not mean I should know better and be able to apply everything that I have learnt to my own mental health.

Ultimately, if you encounter the myth that just

because you're an aspiring or qualified psychologist that you should know better than everyone else, and you should be able to apply your psychological knowledge to your own mental health. Just know that it is the person who is saying this that is wrong and you have done nothing wrong at all.

I hope you get the support you need for your mental health challenges, because you are human, you are great and you'll only come out of this stronger.

Yet no, psychologists should not know better.

WHY SHOULDN'T YOU UNDERESTIMATE THE MENTAL HEALTH IMPACT ON SIBLINGS?

If you've been a long-term reader of my books or listener of The Psychology World Podcast, you might be aware that as an aspiring clinical psychologist, I want to be trained up in Cognitive Behavioural Therapy and a systemic approach. Most probably a form of family therapy.

I really like these approaches to mental health because as far as I'm concerned the cognitive approach helps tackle the biased cognitive processes that enable the development and maintenance of mental health conditions through the person's interpretation of the life event.

The behavioural approach helps us to understand how mental health difficulties can be learnt responses to life stressors, so they can be unlearnt with the right mental health support.

Finally, whilst the cognitive behavioural elements focus on the psychological aspects of mental health, the systemic approach helps to tackle the social causes and factors of the condition. Since the systemic approach proposes that if there is a disruption in the family system then this has a ricochet effect that impacts the rest of the system.

However, within clinical psychology, much less laypeople outside of psychology, I strongly believe that people think that mental health conditions, especially amongst children, only impact the child themselves and their parents. The child is obviously impacted because they are the one with the condition so they are constantly experiencing the psychological distress and other symptoms that the condition causes.

Then the parents are obviously impacted too because they are worried about the child. They want their child to be safe, okay and they want their child to stop being in such psychological distress.

These are how the standard conversations go in clinical psychology lectures and other conversations I have with laypeople about the impacts of mental health.

Very few people mention the impact of mental health conditions on siblings. Which I think is very interesting because siblings are a part of the family system and yet when it comes to clinical conversations with the family the focus is never on the impact of them.

I think this could be because in my experience, siblings are either thought of as extremely close in the rare instances or they are distant and they don't really talk to each other. Therefore, what happens to one sibling never really impacts the other sibling unless they're fighting with each other.

This is not how mental health works, if a sibling or parent has a mental health condition then the entire family system will experience the impact.

Children always feel and hear and know more than adults will ever give them credit for.

An Example of Why You Should Never Underestimate the Impact of Mental Health on Siblings

When the worst of my mental health started in August 2024 because of my rape, I was so depressed, my Post-Traumatic Stress Disorder was going insane and I was jumping and having panic attacks at every single sound. I never felt safe, I was suicidal and everything was going to hell, I went up to see my best friend.

Originally, I went up to for a night to bring them back because another one of our housemates was coming down for the week. Yet two weeks later, I went up to the Midlands to see them for a few days and because this was technically emergency mental health related my best friend already had something planned on the Saturday. So me and their mum went out for the day and I have a lot of time and love for their mum.

She's French and she is lovely, so accepting and she is just a great parent. She has her flaws because who doesn't, but I really like her. And she really likes me.

Anyway, in the afternoon when we were walking the dog (my little shadow), we were talking about mental health approaches. She mentioned that when my best friend was in therapy, there was a family therapy session and my friend's brother mentioned he was feeling really scared and anxious that something was going to happen to his sibling.

My friend's mum was shocked by the statement because during all my best friend's struggles, she had never ever considered that her son had been impacted by this. He was the brother, he didn't have the mental health struggles himself, so it never crossed her mind that it would impact him.

But it really, really did.

He loved my best friend so much like a brother should, so to see my best friend so depressed, struggling so much and being unable to get out of bed for months on end. It really did impact him.

Personally, this was a powerful reminder for me about why I want to be trained up in the systemic approaches because this is important. Mental health always impacts other people, it impacts friends, family and siblings.

Mental health impacts every single level of our social interactions. It impacts the person themselves, their friends, their family, their peers and it impacts society as a whole.

This is why mental health support is so critical and this is why I want to be trained in systemic approaches so I can combine the idea of the family system with the cognitive behavioural elements.

The systemic approaches will help me to add extra tools to my arsenal that I can use to help work with clients to decrease their psychological distress, improve their lives and teach them more adaptive coping mechanisms to deal with life's stressors.

After hearing what my best friend's family went through, I am more determined than ever to get trained in systemic approaches.

I want to help people as much as I can and if learning systemic approaches helps me do that then I will happily do it.

What approaches do you want to be trained in?

THE SURVIVOR CONVERSATION

In a strange twisted sort of way, it's funny that every time I think that I am done writing about sexual trauma, something pops up in my life that makes me really, really want to reflect on it. And this is one of those times.

Now, the reason why I'm including this reflection in a clinical psychology book isn't only because sexual trauma even after rape counselling and trauma recovery has major impacts on our clients' mental health. Yet I am also including it because you never know who's going to walk through your therapy door and into your office.

For example, at the time of writing, I've been doing anorexia counselling for about two months and she had no idea she was going to be supporting someone who was raped. She had thought she was meeting someone with anorexia, but because mental health is so tangled with life experiences, she quickly adapted to be supporting a rape survivor too, because my anorexia and rape are connected.

Of course, she had never been trained in sexual trauma counselling or how to support rape survivors. Thankfully, because I've already been through specialist rape counselling, 99% of my rape trauma has been dealt with, processed and healed.

However, I want to include this reflection and the next one because as you'll see a new experience I'm having is playing on and harming my mental health. Therefore, in this reflection, you'll learn some valuable knowledge about rape survivors and live after rape which will help you understand of rape survivors, so your empathy can increase and you'll have a little extra knowledge to be able to support survivors if one ever walks through your door.

Which given how common rape and other forms of sexual violence is in our society that is almost a heartbreaking guarantee.

<u>What Is The Survivor Conversation?</u>

In all fairness, I always call this conversation "The Rape Conversation", and for the purposes of naming this chapter, I was going to call it "The R Conversation". However, I didn't want readers thinking this was going to be about the statistical software R Studio.

Therefore, about two weeks ago, I got into a casual relationship with someone I think is really clever, beautiful and they are a great person. They are really busy and I always have 100s of projects on the go at any one time so when they offered me a casual relationship, I agreed.

In case you don't know what a casual relationship was (like I didn't until two weeks ago), here's a definition:

"a casual relationship is a form of interpersonal relationship that is typically characterized by a relaxed and non-exclusive nature. For example, Tokito is into polyonomy anyway and I am "open-minded" at the very least. Therefore, unlike committed relationships, casual relationships focus on flexibility, mutual enjoyment as well as independence without the expectation of long-term commitment or being exclusive. Also, casual relationships tend to involve physical intimacy and less intense and exclusive emotional connection.

Furthermore, casual relationships can be divided into different types. For example, Friends with Benefits which I did a podcast episode on in April 2024, these focus on the friendship elements and the friends have sex. Then there are "booty calls" that are for people who rarely contact each other and they have last-minute or late night arrangements for sex. Then there are one-night stands, No-Strings-Attached so this only focuses on having sex and minimal personal sharing. As well as there is casual dating where the partners go on dates and be physically intimate but they don't plan for future commitment."

Anyway, the person I am with really likes sex and honestly, I really want to have sex too. I am a virgin, my only sexual experience was my rape and I feel safe with this person. I know that even though they are hypersexual and they love sex, they would never hurt me. We built our relationship and our friendship round our mutual interests and we have never really spoken about sex, but we know a few things about what the other is into sexually.

Nonetheless, I am scared to have the R conversation with them because it means I have to reveal to them a part of my life that I hate more than anything else. I know some people would be confused by that statement because I have written three books about sexual trauma, I am writing this reflection and the next one and I have podcasted a lot about sexual trauma and the impact it has had on my life.

It does not mean I enjoy this at all.

I am scared that if I reveal that I was raped that this person might see that as a dealbreaker, they might see me as more effort than I am worth and they might not want to have sex and do anything physical with me.

In reality, I know the chances of that are very slim, but it is still a concern.

In addition, I am scared about telling someone new because this means that my rape is just a part of who I am from now on. It means whenever I meet someone, whenever I want to have a relationship, whenever I want to do perfectly normal things with a guy or transmasculine individual, I have to explain that I was raped to them.

It breaks my heart that even now after everything I have survived, everything I have cried over and healed from. My rape is still impacting me and it makes me angry.

I am so bloody annoyed that I have to keep dealing with this rape. I never wanted to be raped. I never wanted to meet my rapist that night or any night for that matter. I hate him, I hate what he has done to me and I wish he was dead to be quite frank.

The fact that even after 11 months he is here impacting me. He is still influencing my decisions and he is still impacting my mental health makes me so angry because this is my life and as much as I don't want to, my rape is a small part of who I am.

And I need to deal with this accordingly.

Why The R Conversation Is Important For Clients As Aspiring and Qualified Psychologists?

I just needed to change the music I'm listening to because clearly the music was not helping me to self-soothe as effectively as I would have liked. Yet I learnt long ago never to bottle up my emotions about my stupid rapist, he deserved everything, and it is rare for me to show any emotions towards my rapist because he isn't worth my brain power. Yet I am annoyed at him.

Anyway, I think as aspiring or qualified psychologists, if a client mentions that this is something that is weighing on their mind. I don't think it is helpful to try and dissuade them from telling their partner, but of course have an in-depth conversation with the client about this.

It is important that you understand the client actually wants this for *them* and it isn't because they feel compelled to from an external source. They need to have the R conversation for them and no one else.

Additionally, I think it's important to have this conversation whenever the client is comfortable, because ideally, they will have it earlier in the relationship because if it is a dealbreaker then the sooner they have it, the better. Yet it is best not to have it too early in the relationship because as I am finding out, wanting to have the R conversation is very draining emotionally and it wreaks havoc on their mental health over time.

Lastly, before I move on, it is important that the client allows themselves to have this conversation. Otherwise, it will play on their mind, it will eat away at them and it will not be helpful to their mental health.

I first mentioned the Rape conversation to my housemates the week I asked this person out, and one of my housemates was like "it's playing on your mind so you should tell them,"

And because I want to start being physical with this person and I don't get to see them often, because we are both so busy and we are in a casual relationship. I want to have this conversation as soon as possible. As well as we have been talking and we have developed a good friendship for months, so they know me.

The night we decided to get into a relationship, they point-blank said I'm great.

This is why I want to have the rape conversation,

I want to do it now so I can move past this mental block and hopefully feel better about wanting to do physical stuff with my partner.

Side note: I understand that the idea of a casual relationship seems weird to people, and in an upcoming book I talk and research casual relationships in a lot more depth. Yes, I am *that* sort of autistic person that flat out loves researching things that they don't understand.

However, after being raped and after being abused for a decade by intensely homophobic people so much so that I have been in fear for my life every day during that period. I have never been in a relationship, never had sex, never done anything. If anything else, I want to use a casual relationship as a learning experience.

If it works that is brilliant, if not, then I would have learnt a lot and hopefully had some fun experiences along the way.

How I Want To Have The R Conversation and The Scaling Question

Later in this section, I'll use one of my favourite counselling techniques to help me focus on the most likely reaction to the rape conversation, but I want to talk about how I want to have the rape conversation.

I firmly believe that when it comes to having such an emotional conversation, it is very important that the survivor controls the situation. It is important that they feel safe, secure and like they are in no danger whatsoever.

This is why I have three different situations in mind.

In an ideal world, me and my partner are meant to be going on a date this afternoon, but they haven't replied to my text to confirm it yet. Of course, if our date doesn't happen, I will be disappointed but because this is sort of what I signed up for. In the sense that this is a brand-new relationship, we agreed to keep it casual and we are both busy.

As well as I am spending all afternoon and evening with them tomorrow.

Anyway, if our date happens then I will have the conversation at the bar we're going to go to on campus. It will be in a public space that I am familiar with, I am with the person I really like and the person who would never hurt me and I am at the university. I have always felt safe at the University of Kent so this will be a place that I control completely.

Secondly, if our date doesn't happen then I have two options for tomorrow. The most probable option because I want to get this conversation over and done with, especially because it is so emotional, I want to spend time with my partner afterwards.

As a result, we spend the afternoon playing Dungeons and Dragons with our friends and there are breaks. So during one of the breaks, me and my partner will likely go off together like we do from time to time and as we're walking to the Co-Op or somewhere else to grab coffee, I'll bring it up. Or at the particular place where my partner likes to grab coffee, there are tables so I might say something like "hey, can we sit down for a few minutes? I want to tell you something important,"

I would prefer that option because then me and my partner can go back to playing Dungeons and Dragons and I can see that I haven't ruined the relationship.

Thirdly, and this is the worst option in my opinion but if this is what needs to happen then it happens. I'll tell my partner that I was raped when I drop them off back at their university accommodation at the end of the night.

Personally, I don't really like this option because it is right at the end of the night. I cannot see them processing it too much and I don't want to spend the next week panicking that I've messed up my relationship by having the R Conversation.

In reality, I know the chances of that are tiny but still, my brain used to be that cruel to me so it might be again. I do not know.

Finally, the best option in my opinion, even though I will probably go for the second option, is after playing Dungeons and Dragons me, my partner and two of our other friends (there are more that we play with but they aren't coming), we're coming back to my shared university house to play games for a few hours and have dinner.

Now, ideally, I want to say to my partner, something along the lines of "hey, can I talk to you upstairs for a few minutes? It's important and I can show you my really cool audio booth too,"

Personally, I really do want to show them my audio booth because they are interested in all my different projects and it's one of the reasons they find me really cool too.

I want to tell them in my room because whilst my bedroom was a source of agony, trauma and nightmares during the worst of my sexual trauma. I wasn't raped in my bedroom but it represented a lot of awful things for me that connected to my rape. Now it is a space that I love because it is where I create my podcast, I write, I create my stories and so on.

My bedroom is somewhere I fully control, and I have had one of my housemates in here before for hours whilst we just talked about life, love and sex. So I am comfortable having other people in here so I am happy.

All of these four situations involve places where I feel safe and in control. Two concepts that are flat out critical for survivors.

Therefore, during all these different possible situations, I would say something along the following lines:

"Hey, I presume at some point, we'll get physical. And believe me, I want to do things with you, but you know I'm a virgin so we need to go slow because of that. But also… I was raped (or I am a rape survivor) so we need to bear that in mind,"

Then the rest of the conversation depends on

their response.

It is that response that I am nervous about and that's why for the last section of this reflection, I want to use the Scaling Question. Basically, you come up with three situations, one that is most likely, one that is more extreme and the last one that is worst case scenario. Then you think about each one in turn.

I think knowing my partner, the most likely response from my partner is surprise, shock and an "I'm sorry you went through that". I think this because my partner is very sexual but they are very clever, very understanding and they are good. And they are aware of mental health things because we have had general conversations about how mental health works in the past and we have dipped into each other's mental health without too much depth.

This would be the best-case scenario because it wouldn't be the end of our relationship and it means my partner would be aware of my sexual trauma, and when we get to doing physical things, we could bear that in mind.

A worse scenario is my partner recoils and they say something like they need to think about this, and they are overwhelmed in shock and horror and they need to think about what this means.

Even writing this, I have to laugh a little because my partner is not like that in the slightest. They know me, we formed our friendship and then relationship through our shared interests and they have hookups so they can always get sex through other means. They are with me casually because as they said “I’m great” and we have a lot of shared interests.

We talk for hours every week whenever we get together. Sex has never come up before.

Leading me onto the last worst-case scenario, and this is what scares me about the rape conversation. I am scared that my partner will see me as a broken, wreck who cannot have sex and that I will be too much effort for them. They might not want to go slow round sex, they might not want to have to think about what they are allowed to do and not because they are used to casual and meaningless hookups.

What if I am too much effort for them?

Honestly, I think that again this comes back to what our relationship was started by. We might have a brand-new relationship that is casual in nature so it isn’t very deep and it isn’t exclusive. Yet they like me for me, they are always happy to talk to me and they always want to talk to me. We make each other laugh, smile and have a great time together.

Our relationship and friendship is more than sex so even if that is true (which it is not) then we can still have a more platonic relationship as much as I want to do physical stuff with them. As well as if they need time to process stuff then I’ll give it to them.

Finally, I am Connor Whiteley. A psychology student, a friend, a podcaster, an international bestselling author, a researcher, a student ambassador, a rape survivor and on and on and on.

I am so many things and I know my core values of creativity, supportive, independence, lifelong learning and curiosity. As nice and lovely as relationships are, I do not need a relationship to define me or make me whole.

Conclusion

Whilst there was a lot more to process than I thought I am really happy that I did and I want to thank you amazing readers for giving me the opportunity to reflect with you.

In terms of future clinical work, if you ever work with a survivor who is concerned about starting a new relationship because they will have to have the rape conversation at some point. Then hopefully this reflection and my comments on control, feeling safe and use the scaling question will help you support that client a little better.

Being a rape survivor should never define anyone and it most certainly shouldn't stop people from feeling loved, supported and being in a relationship.

Sometimes we just require a little extra support and guidance and that is something that you, an aspiring or qualified psychologist, can help improve lives for the better.

HOW DID THE "I AM A SURVIVOR" CONVERSATION GO?

Towards the end of the reflection, I'll explain why this topic is important to be aware of in clinical psychology, but after I wrote the last reflection, it really did help me for a few hours because I texted my partner about if we were going on our date around 1 pm and they wanted a rain check. The crazy person had stayed up for two days straight trying to get ahead on work and they promised to catch up with me about it the next day, which we did.

However, to my surprise, my mental health slightly dipped in the early afternoon. I didn't dip in the morning because I went to my housemate's atomic physics lecture, which turned into a chemistry lecture which was interesting.

I did not understand any of it but it was interesting.

However, when I got back to my house, it was really hard to focus, I was a little anxious and I couldn't stop thinking about the rape conversation that I needed to have with my partner. I really didn't expect my mental health to start dipping, because I had been fine the night before and I was okay.

I learnt during my rape counselling that when this happens and I start to ruminate on my rape or rape-related topics, I need to do something. Therefore, I started writing a psychology article on *What Is Media Psychology* for the next episode of The Psychology World Podcast. I put in my wireless earphones too and blasted some Demonslayer anime music to help drown out the rape thoughts.

Normally, this works for me because it's self-soothing, it calms me down and it keeps my mind busy and when I finish my brain has moved on from whatever was troubling me.

It didn't work this time.

I got to about 1,200 words of the article and I just couldn't write anymore because I was focusing way too much on my anxiety about having this rape conversation.

Thankfully, at that point, my best friend was downstairs making lunch and they hadn't been having a good morning so I wanted to check on them. Also, my best friend is very easy to play. When they're down and depressed, the best thing for them is to give them a problem to focus on.

They might lack self-awareness but they love

helping others so they don't have to focus on themselves. And again, it helps to distract them and they felt a lot better afterwards.

As a result, I ran them through a lot of what I wrote in the last reflection about my concerns, my fears and how I wanted to have this conversation. My best friend understood it and it was really helpful talking to them because the best piece of advice was do not tell your partner that you want to talk to them beforehand because that puts them on edge.

Yes, I do know I should have known that, but this is new to me I swear.

Finally for this section, whilst talking with my best friend helped me until I went to bed, I didn't sleep well that night. I only slept in two-hour chunks because I would wake up just thinking and being anxious about how the rape conversation would go.

The Conversation Itself

I arrived at the Dungeons and Dragons game an hour late because I was working at the university and that was planned. I sat next to my best friend and they were confused that I wasn't sitting next to my partner. Yet I wanted to see my best friend and my partner had stuff on their chair.

Next time I need to sit next to them though, it was slightly sensory overload for my best friend being trapped between me and my partner whilst we talked in game.

Anyway, it was a lovely day all told and then there was a break and what I really liked about me and my partner dating is that we naturally work together. My partner mentioned wanting a drink in the Co-Op and as everyone left and we finished up conversations, we slowly went over to each other and left together.

Then we went to Co-Op talked about life, my partner brought up dating and when we were on the way back I said "as we're dating, you should know 11 months ago, I was raped,"

My partner was surprised and taken aback a bit because that is a hell of a statement to say, but my partner was understanding. They nodded and they revealed something to me so they were very, very understanding.

For the rest of the night, it was lovely, and this was why I wanted to have the conversation earlier in the day if possible. It allowed me and my partner to simply talk, have fun and just spend time together without me worrying that I had made a mistake telling them. Or even worse, my worrying that they had said they were fine with me being a rape survivor but because we couldn't spend time together and I could see for myself that nothing was different between us that I would worry.

Thankfully, I noticed there was something a little different between us. Partly I think this was because this was the first time we had seen each other since we got together properly, but we were a little more couple-y and it was lovely.

We talked, teased each other and I noticed how

much my partner likes talking to me. Which surprised me because I noticed how much slower they talk with me compared to other people, they mocked me for asking permission to hug them and they stopped outside their accommodation for 30 minutes because they wanted to keep talking to me.

And when I asked how could we make Saturdays (our main days of seeing each other) more datey, they were the first to suggest hanging out after our DnD hours at my place and they may or may not stay the night.

Overall, this allowed me to see that my partner didn't see me as a broken, wrecked person who was raped. It allowed me to see that my partner likes me for me and they understand that I was raped so I have some trauma, and they're willing to work with and support me if things pop up.

Applying This Information To Clinical Psychology

The reason why I'm telling you all this is because after experiencing trauma and whenever it comes to mental health conditions, it is perfectly natural for clients to be anxious. As well as if I had had a counselling session last week, I would have spoken to my counsellor about this issue.

She isn't a rape specialist but she is a mental health professional, and as a client, I expect her to be able to help me. Therefore, you might think that you will never ever meet a sexual violence survivor in your life, but chances are that you will.

I want you to be prepared, even a little, with

some extra information that might help you support a client a little better.

Of course, nothing in this book is ever any sort of official advice and you will always know your client best, but you might want to mention that you've read that my experience went well. So there is a chance that a client's conversation could go well too.

In addition, this is why I like scaling questions because it allows you to see if fears and anxieties are based in reality or not.

Another reason I'm telling you this is because I'm really happy that after being raped, after losing 2024 to my mental health and after almost killing myself a few times in 2024, I am just grateful to be alive with my friends and my business and writing intact. And now I have my first-ever partner.

As another friend texted me yesterday, these are exciting times for sure and I no longer have to be anxious about the rape conversation.

My mind is free now to enjoy the relationship and I fully intend to take advantage of that fact as time goes on.

WHY IS THE BODY MASS INDEX STUPID?

In the interest of giving you a full understanding about the research, professional opinions and facts about why doctors are moving away from the Body Mass Index (BMI) as a way of indicating how healthy you are, I'll include a short psychology article that I wrote in 2022 on the topic.

However, before that, I want to reflect on my anger, my rage and my sheer frustration at the BMI as an indicator of health. Since back in November 2024, my anorexia was in full-swing, my housemates were deadly stressed about my lack of eating, my weight loss and my best friend was constantly scared to death that I was going to die.

As a result, after a lot of toing and throwing, I agreed to schedule a doctor's appointment and I went. Yet he said I was fine, I didn't have anorexia and he wasn't going to do anything because my BMI was fine for my weight and height. That is a useless indicator of health given I was telling him how exhausted I was, how sick I was making myself and how poor my eating habits were.

But oh no, because the almighty BMI said I was fine, I did not have anorexia. My weight was perfectly okay and I wasn't experiencing any mental health difficulties.

I did not receive any treatment for my anorexia. This led to a very unfortunate habit that I convinced myself that I *needed* to get worse so I could receive help. I talk more about the other factors in my book, *Anorexia and Me*, but I was tired of "professionals" saying that I didn't have anorexia.

I reduced my calorie intake even more, I avoided complex carbs with a vengeance and I skipped even more meals. My weight loss continued and my anxiety and distress around eating only increased and as you can expect, I got sicker and sicker because of it.

Still, I was fine because my BMI said I was okay so my health was nothing to be worried about.

As a result, this is what annoys me about health services in the United Kingdom, England in particular, because mental health services are so well-protected. I cannot speak to someone who actually understands mental health, anorexia and I can only talk to a medical professional so is severely overworked.

And yes, I am well aware that everyone in the

NHS is extremely overworked, understaffed and underpaid.

Nonetheless, I think if I had been able to talk to a psychologist then I might have felt more validated, supported and even if I wasn't clinically severe enough to warrant NHS treatment. The psychologist might have said something that made me feel like my only option wasn't to get dramatically worse and try to lose even more weight.

After I left the doctor's on this particular day, I did the particular anorexia behaviour (for the first time) of buying laxatives and I took eight of them. So if I was even asked the question about "have you ever tried to make yourself sick before" I could say yes this time. As well as someone might actually believe me when I say I have anorexia.

If the doctor had just trusted me, validated me and used other health indicators instead of the BMI then maybe my anorexia wouldn't have gotten as bad as it did.

Below is a fascinating psychology article to help you understand the stupidity of the BMI in more depth. Enjoy.

<u>Why Are Doctors Moving Away From BMI?</u>

Personally, this doesn't surprise me that this is happening within the medical field. Since if you've done clinical psychology before, this is a subset of arguments that I learnt about recently. There were a lot of problems with the BMI, and we will talk about these, but I do welcome the vote by the American

Medical Association to move away from the BMI.

In addition, in case you're new to Body Mass Index, this is the formula where a person's weight in Kilograms is divided by the square of their height in metres. Then the result of this formula is classified into one of four categories. They are:

- Underweight
- Normal weight
- Overweight
- Obese

These labels aren't rare in the US medical system, and as someone from the UK, I regularly hear these labels too.

However, what is really interesting is the history behind the BMI because once you know the history of this formula then you really start to question why on Earth it's used in medicine in the first place. It isn't based on evidence at all.

What Is The History of The BMI?

The weird thing about the BMI is that it was invented in the 1830s by a Belgian statistician because they wanted to describe the "average man". I suppose that is fine fair enough because we all want to research and describe things from time to time.

Nonetheless, it rose to popularity in the medical field during the 1970s by the physiologist Ancel Keys. Since he was looking for a better way for the US health insurance companies to estimate a person's body fat. The theory behind this is that there is a correlation between someone's body fat and the risk of them dying.

In other words, he wanted to make it more effective for US health insurance to charge people more money if they had more body fat.

Now as someone from the UK, and I don't doubt the US health insurance companies will sadly move into this country in my lifetime. I think this is awful, crazy and harsh, because I have only ever heard of horror stories from Americans about their insurance companies.

Anyway, the BMI was a much better and simpler calculation for finding out someone's body fat compared to the methods used by the US health insurance companies at the time.

Furthermore, to be fair, we have to admit that the BMI is very useful at evaluating large populations, but it is a lot less helpful for evaluating a single person's health. The reason for this is because there is no way at all to quantify a person's muscle and bone mass so athletes tend to have higher BMIs because of their higher muscle mass. Yet according to the BMI, they might be overweight.

Another example is that as a person ages, they lose muscle mass and increase abdominal fat and this unhealthy change isn't picked up by the BMI.

A third problem is that the BMI was mainly developed as well as tested on white men. Yet a person's body composition varies massively between genders, ethnicities and races. For example, a perfectly healthy black woman might appear to be overweight or even obese according to the BMI.

This is why the BMI is a rather useless metric if we really look into it.

Tomiyama et al. (2016)

Whilst there are a lot of studies that investigate the sheer amount of people that are miscategorised by the BMI, I do want to focus on this particular study. Due to this particular one actually compared the BMI against other measures of health. Including, blood pressure, insulin resistance, glucose, cholesterol and a few others in over 40,000 adults.

The results demonstrated nearly half of the "overweight" people as well as 30% of the "obese" people actually had healthy metabolism.

Moreover, more than 30% of the people with a so-called normal weight had an unhealthy metabolism. Therefore, if you take this number and apply it to the US population then this means that there are over 74 million people in the US that are misclassified as unhealthy or healthy according to the BMI.

As a result, whilst the BMI isn't perfect and I believe it has very, very limited uses, the American Medical Association doesn't want to resign it to history. Instead they want doctors to use other factors to determine someone's health like those used in the study above. And this is a very good quote from American Medical Association Immediate Past President Dr Jack Resneck:

"There are numerous concerns with the way BMI has been used to measure body fat and diagnose obesity, yet some physicians find it to be a helpful measure in certain scenarios. It is important for physicians to understand the benefits and limitations of using BMI in clinical settings to determine the best care for their patients."

Conclusion

At the end of this podcast episode, I have to admit that I really am going through a biological psychology phase at the moment for a reason I flat out don't understand. Yet I wanted to do this podcast episode because I heard about the disadvantages of the BMI but I haven't looked into them in any depth until now.

I understand why the BMI isn't a great tool and I really hope that medical doctors do start to walk away from the BMI properly.

And to bring this back to psychology, as much as I hate this, I truly, truly hate this. Since the American Psychological Association has a lot of medical input, the BMI requirements for a lot of eating disorders will not be replaced with something more useful to psychologists until the medical doctors get rid of it themselves.

This is another reason why we need to move beyond diagnosis like I've done previous podcast episodes on.

Anyway, until that happens, we will have to put with the BMI for a little bit longer and we can start to slowly use other measures of body fat in the meantime.

But this is certainly a step in the right direction.

Health Psychology References

Caleyachetty, R., Meunnig, P., & Kengne, A. P. (2016). Misclassification of cardiometabolic health when using body mass index categories. *International Journal of Obesity*, *40*(8), 1332-1332.

Goh, K. C., Safonov, M. G., & Papavassilopoulos, G. P. (1994, December). A global optimization approach for the BMI problem. In *Proceedings of 1994 33rd IEEE Conference on Decision and Control* (Vol. 3, pp. 2009-2014). IEEE.

Rothman, K. J. (2008). BMI-related errors in the measurement of obesity. *International journal of obesity*, *32*(3), S56-S59.

Tomiyama, A. J., Hunger, J. M., Nguyen-Cuu, J., & Wells, C. (2016). Misclassification of cardiometabolic health when using body mass index categories in NHANES 2005–2012. *International journal of obesity*, *40*(5), 883-886.

Why Doctors Are Moving Away from BMI | Psychology Today

UPDATED THOUGHTS ON THE BIOMEDICAL MODEL

Building upon the last reflection, I wanted to take this opportunity to share my updated thoughts on the biomedical model after my recent medical experience for my anorexia. This will be a shorter reflection but it is still important to reflect on, and more importantly, how this might impact my own future clinical work.

After what my doctor did by dismissing my anorexia and completely invalidating my experience because biologically I was fine according to him, this has only made me hate the biomedical model even more.

It is just so frustrating, so maddening and so annoying that just because from a biological standpoint my weight was so-called healthy according to a flawed Body Mass Index, and he thought I looked okay. That I was denied help.

It would have been even slightly better if he had said you probably do have subclinical anorexia but not severe enough for me to refer you. That might have been slightly better because at least he wouldn't have been yet another professional saying I was okay when I was really wasn't.

In addition, if he had only considered the psychological and social information I was telling him. I told him about my lack of eating, how I was scared to eat and gain weight and how my rape trauma had amplified my anorexia. As well as I told him I was losing a kilogram a week without fail.

Still, he said I was fine and he didn't care to think about the psychological and social factors (more like red flags) that I was telling him.

This just goes to show how stupid the biomedical model is, because if the medical doctor had only listened to the other information I was telling him then maybe I could have been helped. Maybe I could have felt supported so I didn't get worse and restrict my eating even more to the point where I got so sick that I wasn't able to do much.

I hate the biomedical model and this is why we must always try to follow more holistic models, like the biopsychosocial model. And yes, I know in the real world, I have been informed that this model is used as the bio-bio-bio model because it is still the biological factors that are the focus.

Yet we need to move past this ancient, dangerous and useless thinking.

Personally, in my future clinical work, this is a difficult one because once a client has already got to me. They would have been through the numerous gatekeepers designed to make sure only the people with the most severe and deadly mental health conditions get through to mental health services.

I'll return to that point in a moment.

Nonetheless, in terms of my personal work, this is a good reminder that I need to always acknowledge multiple factors. Mental health difficulties are never caused by a single factor or type of factor. There might be a main overarching causal factor, but it will still be supported or propped up by smaller factors too.

For example, if we look at my social anxiety after my rape, this was mainly caused by my Post-Traumatic Stress Disorder with my intrusive thoughts, and my anxiety around getting raped again. Yet it was also propped up by the physical sensations I was experiencing, my learnt response that if I went out by myself then I would have a mental crisis when I came back and so on.

I always need to remember mental health difficulties aren't caused by a single factor. That is way too reductionist for the real world.

Moreover, circling back to my appointment about gatekeepers, in an ideal world, I would try and bring about some kind of change so psychology can be involved in primary mental health care. In the last Clinical Psychology Reflection book, I wrote about the Lanson Model in Cornwall that I flat out love.

If I ever see a job advertised based on this model so I can work with people with mental health difficulties instead of them seeing a medical doctor, then I will try to take it. I fully believe that is the future of mental health care as a first line of defence and it is insanely valuable

And it might have helped me, so I want to help other people.

What are your thoughts on the biomedical model?

LEARNING FROM FAILURE IN PSYCHOLOGY

Failure is a part of life and for psychology students and aspiring psychologists, failure is just a part of the psychology journey. Of course, it is not a fun part of the journey and failure tends to be a force that knocks us down. Yet what's most important is how we bounce back from any failures that we experience.

This is called resilience and I've written a lot about psychological resilience and how to increase it, so if you want to learn more, please check The Psychology World Podcast and my books.

In this reflection, I want to reflect on the importance of learning from failure on your psychology journey. I'll start by reflecting more generally then I'll explain how you can learn from failed assignments, failed social relationships and failed applications.

Those three examples will all be common examples amongst aspiring psychologists.

Learning From Failure

Personally, I am a massive believer in learning from failure because there are two aspects of this learning. Firstly, you can do what I call "failure to succeed". You might fail to succeed if you're doing a task and you want to get so much done and you fall short of your goals. But as you have still done something, you have actually succeeded to some extent as you managed to do more than before.

A psychology example is you have a 3,000-word essay and you wanted to write it in two weeks. By the end of the two weeks, you "only" manage 2,000 words. That is a failure because you didn't manage to complete the assignment, but you still managed to do 2,000-words in two weeks. That is a lot more words than you had two weeks ago.

I am always dealing with these sort of failures because whether it is psychology, personal or business related I am always giving myself too much to do. This means by the end of the week (because I do myself weekly To Do Lists), I have often only done between 75% and 90% of my To Do List. Yet instead of berating myself, judging myself harshly and thinking of myself as a failure, I focus on everything I did do.

This is something you can use in your own psychology journey, you can learn from your failures by using the mindset of "failed to succeed,".

On the other hand, you can always learn from failure because there is always a reason why you fail, or multiple reasons. It might be because you thought you had more time than you did, you didn't know how to do something, you weren't disciplined enough with your time and so on.

As much as you might not want to look back on the reasons of your failure, it is useful if you do. It gives you a chance to learn, so you can improve next time.

A personal example is it took me an extra month to write an academic paper than I wanted to. If I had done the academic paper sooner then my time would have been a lot more free, it would have been one less major project on my mind and I would have been relieved.

I still kept putting it off every week for a month. In other words, I kept failing to finish off this paper.

When I looked back at the reasons why I kept failing, it was down to three main factors:

- I lacked motivation because I knew it wouldn't take me long to do it.
- I wasn't disciplined enough with my time.
- I gave myself too many other things to do so the academic paper wasn't the priority.

This is why towards the end of last week when I actually finished the academic paper, I showed more discipline so I could learn from my previous failures. I set a date and time that I was going to work on this paper and I wasn't going to do anything else in this time no matter how badly I wanted to.

How To Learn from Failed Assignments?

Building upon my last example, there will always be times when aspiring psychologists don't do as well on an assignment as they hoped they would. This was the story of my first two years of my undergraduate degree. My academic writing was awful, I couldn't do well on any assignments and if I didn't have my placement year where a lecturer and his PhD student sat me down and taught me academic writing. I very well might have failed my degree.

Or you can fail assignments outright.

As a result, it's important that you learn from your "failures" if you don't do as well as you wanted to or you outright fail an assignment. If you do this then you'll be able to apply what you learnt going forward so you can do better, and achieve the grades that you want to.

Of course, unfortunately, this is not as easy as it might first appear. I know at my university, markers do not give very useful feedback because they are only paid for 40 minutes per assignment. It takes at least an hour and a half to mark an assignment and give good feedback. Therefore, they don't give good feedback because they don't want to work for free.

There is a major payment issue here and that is negatively impacting students' ability to improve.

However, there are other ways how you can learn from your failure when it comes to university assignments. Firstly, your lecturer will probably have Office Hours. These are weekly slots where students can come in, talk to the lecturer and ask any questions that they have. You could use this time to get them to talk about your assignment once it's marked and so on.

Hopefully, that would give a lot of feedback and useful suggestions for the future.

Equally, another option is most universities run workshops and have resources to help you with whatever you are struggling with. I should have taken more advantage of this as a student in the first two years of my undergrad. I should have gone to academic writing workshops.

Make sure you look at what your university offers so you can get the help you need to improve and learn from your assignments.

Finally, your university might have a student advisory service or something similar where you can book a one-on-one appointment where people go through your work, answer any questions and so on with you. This is essentially tailored-made support for you. Again, this is something I should have used more in my undergrad degree.

How To learn from Failed Social Relationships?

I wanted to include this next section in this reflection because as aspiring psychologists, we are going to experience a lot of social relationships in our lives. You are going to make friends, make good connections within your cohorts and lecturers and you are going to hopefully find love if you're looking for it.

On the other hand, you are going to go through a lot of heartbreak and failed social relationships. And considering forming relationships with clients and our peers is actually a fundamental part of psychology I think, this is an important area of failure to briefly look at.

Therefore, I firmly believe that you can always learn from failed relationships. There are a handful of major failures in my social relationships that I can think about and I have learnt a lot from them. This is a little painful for me to write about but a few years ago, I was friends for 6 brilliant weeks with a guy who helped me realise that my child abuse was impacting me severely, it was ruining my life and he was amazing.

However, this was the guy I developed emotional dependence with so our friendship became toxic, intense and it wasn't nice for either one of us. Yet I did learn a lot from that friendship, I learnt that I needed to go to counselling to deal with child abuse and that really did help me.

A final example is with a more recent friend who has stopped talking to me. He was always busy with his other friends and boyfriend anyway even when we were talking daily, but during the worst of my anorexia I asked for a little too much support that damaged our relationship.

There are other examples too that were not wrecked by my mental health. For example, don't overshare, don't be too intense and do a number of other autistic traits.

However, it just goes to remind us that as much as the end of friendships, peer relationships and romantic relationships hurt us. And believe me, I know how painful they can be, it's important that we take a little bit of time to learn from the failures.

Here are some questions that you might find helpful:

- Did we do anything worse or did they do something wrong?
- How could we avoid ending up in a similar situation again? (No, never finding friends or love again is not an option)
- What could you do to work on yourself if you caused the failed relationship?

How To Learn from Failed Applications?

The final area I want to focus on in this reflection comes from one of the biggest issues facing aspiring psychologists. This is the issue about being rejected for different job roles, different postgraduate courses and anything else that we get rejected for on our psychology journey.

Whenever you get rejected for a job role, it is not ideal, it is not nice and you tend to feel bad. You might even experience feelings of self-doubt, and you might believe that you're useless as well as you will never become a psychologist.

After those self-critical thoughts go and you're more able to take a step back from the situation, take a deep calming breath and look at what happened. Sometimes organisations will give you a little bit of feedback, which can be really useful.

Yesterday my best friend was telling me how our Outreach department at my university (not psychology related but still) emailed them denying them for a job role. It wasn't because they had done anything wrong, they had aced everything but Outreach didn't want to put too much strain on my best friend because they were applying for other job roles.

Whilst it wasn't the most useful advice, it was helpful because it meant my best friend wasn't at fault here and they could hopefully get the job again next year.

Nonetheless, not all organisations are going to do that automatically. If this happens then you can email them back being polite and asking for feedback. They might give you some, they might not. If you don't ask for feedback then you are never going to get it and you are never going to get the opportunity to learn from this failure.

Lastly, you could review your application. You could really look at it and pretend to be the employer and look if you actually hit the criteria and if the wording was the best it possibly could be. For example, if the job role was about working in a children and adolescent mental health service, you might need to check if your application focuses on children and adolescent mental health services. Or did you mainly focus on adult mental health without linking it back to children and adolescence to show you have transferable skills?

It is doing activities like that that will really help you to learn from your failures.

Ultimately, I don't like the term "failure" because it is negative, it makes you feel bad about yourself and it isn't helpful. Instead, you should see every "failure" or "step back" as a chance to learn and do better next time.

As long as you keep going forward and you never stop, you will never fail. You will hopefully only get better over time.

WE ALL HAVE AT LEAST ONE PREJUDICE

Two days ago, in my clinical psychology module, I had a brilliant lecture on cross-cultural factors in clinical work. It was an interesting lecture looking at how different experiences, ethnic backgrounds and how racism, prejudice and discrimination could impact mental health as well as therapeutic work.

This is especially important for aspiring and qualified psychologists to understand because we need to understand that we are the experts in psychological theory and practice. Yet we will never ever begin to understand how people from different cultures and mixed identities experience the world. For instance, a client might be born in the same country as us but if they have a dual identity, like African American or British-French or British-Thai then these other identities and cultural factors will have an impact on their lived experiences. They might have experienced additional barriers, prejudices and discrimination that we do not.

This all impacts our work with the client.

Therefore, as aspiring and qualified psychologists, we need to understand that we need to be aware of these additional cultural factors, and we need to be preceptive and willing to listen and learn from clients.

I firmly believe that every client can teach us something about ourselves, the world and mental health.

Furthermore, during the lecture, the lecturer showed us a video of his old mentor and the mentor said a very interesting line that really struck me. It was something along the lines of "we all have at least one prejudice,"

As a result, this is something that I want to reflect on in this chapter, because yes, it can be argued that having any form of prejudice is bad. And it is. Ideally, we should live in a world that is free of prejudice and discrimination.

However, unfortunately, I do not believe that is realistic. Instead, I think it is much more helpful to recognise our prejudice and call ourselves out on them. Not because we are bad people and deeply flawed individuals, but because we are human and we want to improve.

We want to improve ourselves and we want to improve for our clients, our work and the future of our profession.

My Prejudice

In a moment, I'll explain what are the benefits of recognising your own prejudices, but if I am asking you to reflect on yours, it is only fair if I talk about mine. Therefore, my prejudice and my flaw is that I can be a little classist at times. Which is weird considering I am from a low middle-class family in a very deprived area., and some of this comes from abuse and trauma.

Yet classism is not okay and whenever I meet people, have certain interactions and whenever I have to make decisions to include people in activities that are different from myself, I do at times need to catch myself about classism.

When I am being slightly classist, these are always subtle because it can be me doubting someone's abilities or thinking I am better than someone because of where they are from. And that is not okay.

Therefore, instead of hating myself for my prejudice, I acknowledge it, show myself self-compassion and I try to overcome this influence.

Am I always successful?

Probably not, but I honestly try. I try to overcome and recognise my prejudice so I can treat everyone I meet with the same respect, equal chance and kindness that I would like from other people when they learn I am from Medway of all places.

Benefits of Recognizing Your Own Prejudices

In addition, by recognising your own prejudices,

this can contribute to your own personal growth because this can distort your perception of reality and how this influences your decisions. It can even influence your decisions so they don't align with your goals and core values.

As a result, by recognising your prejudices, you can find opportunities to challenge your assumptions, so you can refine your critical thinking skills and learn to evaluate information more accurately as well as objectively.

A second benefit is that it can increase emotional growth because it can help you to explore and probe your emotions. Then exploring your emotions can lead to you to discover unrecognised fears, insecurities and/ or prejudices. Also, whilst exploring emotions can be challenging, it can be a very rewarding experience too as you grow emotionally.

Finally, recognising your own prejudices can be useful in social settings too. This is particularly important for aspiring and qualified mental health professionals because all our work involves social relationships. Whether it is between us and our peers, us and our supervisor or us and our clients. Social relationships are a core part of our great profession.

Moreover, in social settings, it's useful to recognise your own biases so you can improve your own interpersonal skills. Since our biases, like our prejudices, can often lead to miscommunications and misunderstandings. Which isn't great when trying to form relationships including the therapeutic alliance.

Overall, by starting to question as well as probe our beliefs, we can start to have more nuanced understandings of complex issues. Including how cultural factors and lived experiences of having different cultural identities, discrimination amongst other factors can impact mental health. It is our chance as aspiring or qualified professionals to change and grow intellectually and become more open to a diverse range of ideas and perspectives.

None of us will ever know everything about people, mental health and how culture impacts mental health. This is why it is so important to listen to other people that are different from us.

And I'll end this reflection by repeating, I firmly believe every single client can teach us something about ourselves, the world and mental health.

We just need to listen.

YOUR UNSHAKABLE SELF IN CLINICAL PSYCHOLOGY

"As long as I have my unshakable self, I can dig in with both feet with all my might. As long as I know who I am, all my doubts, hesitations, and frustrations will disappear. And no demon on earth can escape my descending blade,"

-Muichiro Tokito, Demonslayer Season 4.

I flat out love this quote and whilst it inspired an entire book, *Your Unshakable Self,* I want to talk about the importance of the quote from a clinical psychology viewpoint. I think the quote can be powerful for all of us in two main ways.

It is powerful for us as aspiring psychologists and it is a useful quote to share with clients in certain situations. More on those two ways in a moment.

However, first of all, I want to dissect the quote a little more from a clinical psychology viewpoint. In terms of our profession, the quote is talking about as you know who are you and as long as you know what you want to achieve, you can dig in when the world throws challenges at you with all your might.

As well as the quote talks about how as long as you know who you are and what you want to achieve, then all your doubts, frustrations and hesitations will disappear.

In my book, *Your Unshakable Self*, I talk about this quote from a mental health and resilience angle too. That is a very helpful way of looking at this quote as well.

Yet when it comes to clinical psychology and the final section of the quote, I like to think it is telling us that as long as we know what we want and who we are then there is no challenge, no issue and no obstacle that we cannot overcome.

We can slay any obstacle we come across.

As A Quote For Clients

The inspiration for this little section came from my anorexia counsellor last week because I finally told her about the quote and she really liked it. Therefore, you might want to tell your clients about this quote because it shows a lot about the importance of resilience, knowing yourself and your emotions and it can be useful in a lot of different therapeutic ways.

For example, after trauma work, rebuilding your sense of self is important and I think it would have been more beneficial for me to focus more on that at the end of my rape counselling. Because I didn't know who I was without mental health difficulties, it was what led to my anorexia.

Moreover, sense of self and knowing who you are is an important aspect of mental health treatment for various conditions. Including anorexia because the Maudsley model is all about getting you to amplify the non-anorexia parts of your Self so they can shine through instead of your anorexia. Since in anorexia, once you understand that there is so much more to you than anorexia, treatment seems less scary and it seems more achievable than before.

Overall, if you ever want to do some sense of self work with a client for life after treatment, especially for trauma survivors, then this quote might be very helpful, useful and insightful for you and your clients.

For Aspiring Psychologists

Firstly, as aspiring psychologists, and even once we are fully qualified, we will face a lot of challenges and rejections and failures. We will not always get the jobs we really want, we will get pass over for promotion and we will not always be able to get onto the postgraduate programmes that we want more than anything else in the world.

However, as long as you know your core values, why you want to be a clinical psychologist and what you want to achieve then you will be okay. For example, if you don't get a specific job that would have really helped you to gain clinical experience, then that's okay because it isn't the end of the world.

Whenever any of us get a rejection or "failure"

like that then we will feel bad and awful for a little while. Also, you will naturally feel frustrated, annoyed and you might even start to doubt yourself and whether you can even become a clinical psychologist.

Nonetheless, if you know who you are and why you want to be a clinical psychologist then that's okay. You can remind yourself of these reasons and the doubts will go away.

Personally, I recently didn't manage to get some work experience that would have been really valuable to my future career. It was annoying because I really wanted it, and because I used to be very self-critical, I started to judge myself. Maybe I wasn't good enough, maybe I shouldn't be a psychologist, maybe I should just give up.

Yet I am a person who values supporting others as a core part of who they are, I love life-long learning and I flat out love being curious. Those are three out of my five core values that I really value so I will not give up, and I will never stop learning more about clinical psychology.

It is just part of who I am so I will not stop trying to build up my clinical experience and trying to become a better aspiring psychologist.

In addition, I want to become a clinical psychologist so I can help people like other mental health professionals have helped me. I am only here today because mental health professionals have supported me dealing with my child abuse, my rape trauma and my anorexia and more. I am here because of my own strength, sheer determination to survive and their support.

I want to give that to other people.

On the whole, because I know who I am, why I am doing this and what I want to achieve, I will not doubt my ability to be a clinical psychologist. It will take a while to get there but I can do it.

No matter what challenge or issue or obstacle pops up in front of me, I will dig in with all my might and nothing will escape my descending blade I slay all the obstacles in front of me.

Here's the quote again as a reminder and maybe you'll read it differently now after this chapter.

"As long as I have my unshakable self, I can dig in with both feet with all my might. As long as I know who I am, all my doubts, hesitations, and frustrations will disappear. And no demon on earth can escape my descending blade,"

CONCLUSION

We've covered a lot of brilliant topics in this volume of Clinical Psychology Reflections. We've looked at how mental health is connected to sex and sexual trauma, how mental health can impact siblings and why someone might start anxiety medication as a last resort, and we've covered everything in between and more.

Personally, these books really remind me why I flat out love clinical psychology, and why I am always reflecting and learning and wanting to know more about mental health. There is only so much we can be taught in our lecture theatres and academic textbooks, and I think the real learning happens in the real world.

The real world is where our clients and mental health difficulties are, after all.

If I didn't reflect and think about the real world and what I've read or encountered then I wouldn't be as passionate, excited and thrilled to be an aspiring psychologist as much as I am. These books always make me excited about my future because mental health really does impact every single level of society and there are so many factors that impact our mental health.

There will always be more to learn about, and there will be more experiences to learn from.

And I think as an aspiring psychologist, and even a qualified psychologist, you might have the best grades, the best research experience and maybe even an impressive resume of clinical psychology work experience. Yet truly, I think unless you are able to reflect, improve and learn from your clients and the world around you then you will only go so far.

Our clients do not exist in a vacuum. Every day our clients go outside or they encounter the world and the world impacts them. The looks they get in the streets, the comments they hear against them and the relationships they have with others, they all happen in the real world.

Therefore, as mental health professionals, we must live and reflect on the real world and our experiences too, so we can help understand our clients and our profession a little more.

At the end of this book, I just want to say a massive thank you for reading, I hope you've enjoyed these reflections and that they got you thinking about these topics too.

And now you have a little more knowledge to help you on your clinical psychology journey. Have a great day everyone and hopefully, I'll see you in another book soon.

https://www.subscribepage.io/psychologyboxset

CHECK OUT THE PSYCHOLOGY WORLD PODCAST FOR MORE PSYCHOLOGY INFORMATION! AVAILABLE ON ALL MAJOR PODCAST APPS.

About the author:

Connor Whiteley is the author of over 60 books in the sci-fi fantasy, nonfiction psychology and books for writer's genre and he is a Human Branding Speaker and Consultant.

He is a passionate warhammer 40,000 reader, psychology student and author.

Who narrates his own audiobooks and he hosts The Psychology World Podcast.

All whilst studying Psychology at the University of Kent, England.

Also, he was a former Explorer Scout where he gave a speech to the Maltese President in August 2018 and he attended Prince Charles' 70th Birthday Party at Buckingham Palace in May 2018.

Plus, he is a self-confessed coffee lover!

All books in 'An Introductory Series':

How To Improve Your Relationships

How Does Ageing Affect Us?

Introduction To Psychotherapies

I Am Not A Victim, I Am A Survivor

Breaking The Silence

Healing As A Survivor

Clinical Psychology and Transgender Clients

Clinical Psychology

Moral Psychology

Myths About Clinical Psychology

401 Statistics Questions For Psychology Students

Careers In Psychology

Psychology of Suicide

Dementia Psychology

Clinical Psychology Reflections Volume 4

Forensic Psychology of Terrorism And Hostage-Taking

Forensic Psychology of False Allegations

Year In Psychology

CBT For Anxiety

CBT For Depression

Applied Psychology

BIOLOGICAL PSYCHOLOGY 3RD EDITION

COGNITIVE PSYCHOLOGY THIRD

EDITION

SOCIAL PSYCHOLOGY- 3RD EDITION

ABNORMAL PSYCHOLOGY 3RD EDITION

PSYCHOLOGY OF RELATIONSHIPS- 3RD EDITION

DEVELOPMENTAL PSYCHOLOGY 3RD EDITION

HEALTH PSYCHOLOGY

RESEARCH IN PSYCHOLOGY

A GUIDE TO MENTAL HEALTH AND TREATMENT AROUND THE WORLD- A GLOBAL LOOK AT DEPRESSION

FORENSIC PSYCHOLOGY

THE FORENSIC PSYCHOLOGY OF THEFT, BURGLARY AND OTHER CRIMES AGAINST PROPERTY

CRIMINAL PROFILING: A FORENSIC PSYCHOLOGY GUIDE TO FBI PROFILING AND GEOGRAPHICAL AND STATISTICAL PROFILING.

CLINICAL PSYCHOLOGY

FORMULATION IN PSYCHOTHERAPY

PERSONALITY PSYCHOLOGY AND INDIVIDUAL DIFFERENCES

CLINICAL PSYCHOLOGY REFLECTIONS VOLUME 1

CLINICAL PSYCHOLOGY REFLECTIONS VOLUME 2
Clinical Psychology Reflections Volume 3
CULT PSYCHOLOGY
Police Psychology

A Psychology Student's Guide To University
How Does University Work?
A Student's Guide To University And Learning
University Mental Health and Mindset

Other books by Connor Whiteley:

Bettie English Private Eye Series
The Landlord Problem
Death of Blackmail
The Good Friday Murder
Three's A Pattern
A Very Private Woman
The Russian Case
A Very Urgent Matter
A Case Most Personal
Trains, Scots and Private Eyes
The Federation Protects
Cops, Robbers and Private Eyes
Just Ask Bettie English
An Inheritance To Die For

The Death of Graham Adams
Bearing Witness
The Twelve
The Wrong Body
The Assassination Of Bettie English
Wining And Dying
Eight Hours
Uniformed Cabal
A Case Most Christmas

Gay Romance Novellas
Breaking, Nursing, Repairing A Broken Heart
Jacob And Daniel
Fallen For A Lie
Spying And Weddings
Clean Break
Awakening Love
Meeting A Country Man
Loving Prime Minister
Snowed In Love
Never Been Kissed
Love Betrays You
Love And Hurt

Lord of War Origin Trilogy:
Not Scared Of The Dark
Madness

Burn Them All

Way Of The Odyssey
Odyssey of Rebirth
Convergence of Odysseys
Odyssey Of Hope
Odyssey of Enlightenment

Lady Tano Fantasy Adventure Stories
Betrayal
Murder
Annihilation
Rising Shadow
Coming of Demons

Agents of The Emperor
Deceitful Terra
Blood And Wrath
Infiltration
Fuel To The Fire
Return of The Ancient Ones
Vigilance
Angels of Fire
Kingmaker
The Eight
The Lost Generation
Hunt

Emperor's Council
Speaker of Treachery
Birth Of The Empire
Terraforma
Spaceguard

The Rising Augusta Fantasy Adventure Series
Rise To Power
Rising Walls
Rising Force
Rising Realm

The Fireheart Fantasy Series
Heart of Fire
Heart of Lies
Heart of Prophecy
Heart of Bones
Heart of Fate

City of Assassins (Urban Fantasy)
City of Death
City of Martyrs
City of Pleasure
City of Power

Lord Of War Trilogy (Agents of The Emperor)
Not Scared Of The Dark
Madness
Burn It All Down

Miscellaneous:
Dead Names
RETURN
FREEDOM
SALVATION
Reflection of Mount Flame
The Masked One
The Great Deer
English Independence

OTHER SHORT STORIES BY CONNOR WHITELEY

Mystery Short Story Collections
Criminally Good Stories Volume 1: 20 Detective Mystery Short Stories
Criminally Good Stories Volume 2: 20 Private Investigator Short Stories
Criminally Good Stories Volume 3: 20 Crime Fiction Short Stories
Criminally Good Stories Volume 4: 20 Science Fiction and Fantasy Mystery Short

Stories
Criminally Good Stories Volume 5: 20 Romantic Suspense Short Stories

Connor Whiteley Starter Collections:
Agents of The Emperor Starter Collection
Bettie English Starter Collection
Matilda Plum Starter Collection
Gay Romance Starter Collection
Way Of The Odyssey Starter Collection
Kendra Detective Fiction Starter Collection

Science Fiction Short Story Collections
Rivetingly Great Stories Volume 1
Rivetingly Great Stories Volume 2
Rivetingly Great Stories Volume 3
Rivetingly Great Stories Volume 4
Rivetingly Great Stories Volume 5

www.ingramcontent.com/pod-product-compliance
Lightning Source LLC
LaVergne TN
LVHW022049200926
848481LV00003B/842
9781918599664